HOW TO

DRINK

LIKE A

MOBSTER

HOW TO

LIKE A

Cocktails Guaranteed to Bring Out
Your Inner Gangster

ALBERT W. A. SCHMID
Foreword by Noah Rothbaum

RED ⚡ LIGHTNING BOOKS

This book is a publication of

Red Lightning Books
1320 East 10th Street
Bloomington, Indiana 47405 USA

redlightningbooks.com

Manufactured in the United States of America

Cataloging information is available
from the Library of Congress.

ISBN 978-1-68435-049-0 (hardback)
ISBN 978-1-68435-050-6 (ebook)

1 2 3 4 5   23 22 21 20 19 18

THIS BOOK IS DEDICATED TO
my godfather,

PHIN SAPPENFIELD

CONTENTS

ONE

Drink Like a Mobster!

TWO

People, Places, and Things

THREE

Cocktail Recipes

FOREWORD

AMERICANS ARE OBSESSED WITH MOBSTERS.

I should qualify that statement by saying we are obsessed with the Hollywood version of wise guys. The real loan sharks, bookmakers, protection providers, and waste management specialists are, of course, truly terrifying, and there is nothing remotely charming about them. Dealing with the real articles would make even the most ardent *Sopranos* fans swear off HBO for good.

But the romanticized versions of real and fictional mobsters are hard to resist. Nathan Detroit in *Guys and Dolls*, Edward G. Robinson in *Little Caesar*, and Chazz Palminteri in *Bullets over Broadway* all play bad guys you find yourself rooting for time and time again—no matter how diabolical the scheme.

Not surprisingly, the link between gangsters and booze has deep roots. A lucrative, heavily taxed industry—confined to the borders of larger society—was the perfect environment for the mob to operate within. Prohibition offered the ultimate opportunity for gangsters to control every facet of the liquor business, from manufacturing to distribution to the sale of illicit cocktails.

But in the same way we turned mob bosses into folk heroes, Prohibition also received a good dose of gloss. Although fancy private clubs and hoity-toity spots catering to the rich as they waited for the dawn of repeal existed, most of America was reduced to buying drinks in alleys and dingy speakeasies. Forget intricate cocktails. Drinkers were lucky if alcohol was potable and not deadly. The Prohibition liquor business was uncomfortably close to the illicit drug trade today; most people drank their liquor as quickly as possible and went on their way.

The truth about Prohibition drinking, however, hasn't impeded the rise of the modern speakeasy. The cloak-and-dagger aesthetic is chic, and clandestine watering holes have popped up in most major cities around the world, regardless if the local culture went through its own period of verboten alcohol consumption. And that's not to mention a number of recent TV shows about the criminal alcohol trade, including *Boardwalk Empire* and *Moonshiners*.

So with all that said, I wasn't particularly surprised when Albert Schmid told me he was working on a book about gangsters and cocktails. In fact, if anything, I was jealous that he had come up with the idea first. Fix yourself a drink and enjoy.

Noah Rothbaum

ACKNOWLEDGMENTS

I WOULD LIKE TO THANK the following:

My wife, Kim, for her love, support, and copyediting; my sons, Tom and Mike, for inspiring me to always do my best.

My parents, Elizabeth Schmid and the late Thomas Schmid, for all their support and advice.

My father-in-law, Richard E. Dunn, for his mentorship and our wonderful conversations.

My siblings and their spouses, Gretchen, Tiffany, Rachel, Justin, Bennett, Ana, Shane, and John, for their support.

My colleagues and friends, especially Al "Ice Pick" Romano, who served as consigliere on this project, and the other instructors and professors in the culinary arts and hospitality management departments at Guilford Technical Community College, including Linda Beitz, Michele Prairie, L. J. Rush, Tom Lantz, and Keith Gardner, who I enjoy working with each day. Samphanh Soxayachanh, I enjoy starting my business day with your smile and happy nature.

My friend and former student Loreal "the Butcher Babe" Gavin, whose enthusiasm is infectious.

My friend Scot "Consigliere" Duval for his friendly counsel.

My friend Deet Gilbert, associate professor at Johnson & Wales University–Charlotte, who shared her thoughts on this project.

My friends Brian and Angie Clute—looking forward to the next trip!

My long-time friend Keith Mellage, godfather to both of my sons.

My colleague and friend Rich Depolt for setting an extraordinary example of team leadership.

My colleague and friend Deb Walsh, Esq., for her energy, enthusiasm, and smile.

My colleagues Dr. Beth Pitonzo and Sheila May for their leadership.

My colleague Dr. Randy Parker, fellow PK, for leading the institution where I work and the good words each time I see you.

The artists who made me laugh, smile, and dance while working on this project: Justin Timberlake, Jimmy Fallon, James Corden, Ellen DeGeneres, Etta James, Frank Sinatra, Alicia Keys, Jay-Z, Dr. Dre, Ice-Cube, Bruno Mars, Michael Bublé, and Snoop Dogg.

MOBSTER LEXICON

Administration The top-level management of a Mafia family.

Associate One who works with a Mafia family but is not a "made" member.

B and A racket The nickname for the beer and alcohol business during Prohibition.

Babbo An idiot, useless associate or a straight citizen who has been duped.

Babysitter A body guard, usually for someone who is betraying the Mafia (a rat) before he or she testifies and enter the Program.

Bagman An associate or soldier who picks up and/or distributes bribe or protection money.

Barone A landlord.

Beef A disagreement between members of a Mafia family or between Mafia families.

Biscuit Handgun.

Borgata A Mafia family.

Boss The head of a Mafia family. Also known as the Don, the old man, and sometimes as the godfather.

Broken (Break) Demoted or knocked down from a position.

Buonanima A salutation meaning "rest his soul."

Button An official member of the Mafia.

Buy (Bought) To bribe.

Cafonei An embarrassment to himself or others, a phony, or someone of low class.

Capo Captain.

Capodecina A captain of ten soldiers.

Capo di tutti capi or **Capo dei capi (boss of all bosses)** Before the Commission, central control was held by a single mobster. This practice was discontinued in 1931 with the founding of the Commission. However, the honorary title was given to the most powerful boss of all the Mafia families.

Caporegime A captain of a large group of soldiers.

Che bruta "How ugly are you?"

Che peccato "What a pity" or "what a shame."

Cleaning To avoid being followed.

Clock To monitor someone's movements and activities.

Comare A Mafia mistress.

Come heavy To attend a meeting carrying a loaded gun.

Compare An associate, close pal, or buddy.

Connected Someone who does business with the Mafia but is not a made member.

Consigliere The adviser of a Mafia family of high rank. Usually on the same level as the underboss reporting directly to and advising the boss.

Contract To order a murder of a specific person.

Cosa nostra Italian for "our thing"—referring to the Mafia.

Crew A group of soldiers under a capo's command.

Crumb A working person—someone who is "legit."

Cugine A young soldier working to be made.

Do a piece of work Murder someone.

Don The leader of a Mafia crime family.

Dough Money.

Do up Slang for murder.

Drop A prearranged location.

Earner Someone who generates income for the Mafia.

Eat alone Someone who is greedy.

Empty suit Someone who has nothing to offer but wants to hang around mobsters.

Enforcer A member of the Mafia who encourages people to cooperate with the family agenda or deals with threats, physical assault, or murder.

Family A Mafia crime unit, usually attached to a city or an area.

Father An old term for the boss or the head of a Mafia family.

Featherbedding Assigning more union workers to a project than are necessary.

Fed Federal agent.

Fence A person who deals in stolen product.

Finger To identify for a hit man the person whom you want eliminated.

Fix To pay law enforcement to allow illegal activity.

Flip To cooperate with law enforcement.

Fogazzi Fake, not real.

Forget about it A term with two meanings (1) It is best for all concerned that we not remember that thing that we discussed before; (2) Someone or something has no chance of success.

Friend of mine The term used when introducing someone who can be vouched for to a made member of the Mafia.

Friend of ours The term used when introducing one made member of the Mafia to another made member of the Mafia.

G A thousand dollars (also known as one grand or one large).

Gabagool Something to eat.

Garbage business (waste management business) Organized crime.

Gat A handgun.

Get a place ready Find a place to bury something or someone.

Godfather A term of endearment and respect for the boss.

Goner Someone who is as good a dead.

Goombah Sicilian slang for "compare"; the plural for **goombah** is **goombata**.

Heat Attention from the media or law enforcement. Also a term for a gun.

Heater A gun.

Heavy Armed and ready for action.

Hit To murder.

Honored society The Mafia.

Hot goods Stolen merchandise.

Ice (1) To kill; (2) To stall or delay.

Jamook An idiot or loser.

Joint Prison.

Knock off To kill.

Knock over To rob.

Lay low To act inconspicuous or stay out of sight.

Legit Legal business.

Loan shark (a Shylock) Someone who loans money at very high interest.

Made A term that indicates a man's "membership" in a family. Generally speaking, the person has completed a murder or two for the boss (which once asked cannot be refused on pain of death) or the person is an earner and has made a lot of money for the family.

Make a marriage Two parties partnering for Mafia business or concern.

Make one's bones Establishing one's credibility by murdering someone.

Mark A person or place targeted for criminal activity.

Mattresses (going to, taking it to, or **hitting the)** Going to war with a rival family. The term comes from laying low and hiding in rooms where mattresses are thrown on the floor.

Men of honor (men of respect) A reference to members of the Mafia; how they might refer to themselves.

Messaggero A messenger or ambassador from one family to another.

Mobbed up Connected to the mob.

Moustache Pete A Prohibition-era term referring to Mafiosi members from the old country.

Muscle To intimidate.

Muscle in To move into someone else's territory, plan, or operation usually by force.

Omertà The Mafia's code of silence. The Mafia will take a contract out on a mobster who violates this code. Or the mobster needs to become a rat.

Pass To commute a contract on someone.

Paying tribute Giving the boss a cut of a deal.

Pinched Arrested by the cops or the feds.

Pop To murder.

Rat Someone who breaks omertà after being pinched.

Rub out To murder.

Shakedown To scare someone or to get money or something of value from them.

Soldier Someone at the bottom level of a Mafia family.

Spring cleaning To get rid of evidence.

Swag Stolen goods.

Swimming with the fishes A murder victim who is dumped into a body of water is said to be "swimming with the fishes." The victim may have a cement coffin, cement overcoat, or cement shoes. In other words, the victim's body is encased (in part or in whole) in cement so that the person sinks in the water.

The book(s) The roll of made members of the Mafia. Usually, this is not actually written down, but it is still referred to as the book.

The Commission (the Five Families) Founded in 1931 as a replacement for the **Capo di Tutti Capi**. Today, the Commission consists of at least twenty-one families, but only six have seats on the Commission, including the Bonanno family, the Chicago Outfit, the Colombo family, the Gambino family, the Genovese family, and the Lucchese family. The Genovese family represents the interests of the crime families from Buffalo, Cleveland, Detroit, New England (Patriarca family), New Jersey (the DeCavalcante family), New Orleans, Philadelphia, and Pittsburgh. The Chicago Outfit represents the interests of the crime families from Kansas City, Los Angeles, Milwaukee, San Francisco, San Jose, St. Louis, and Tampa (the Trafficante family).

The nut The bottom line.

The Program The Federal Witness Protection Program.

Underboss The title of the second in command for a Mafia family.

Whack To kill or murder; also bump off, burn, clip, hit, or pop.

Wise guy A made man in the mafia.

HOW TO

LIKE A

"I'm gonna make him an offer he can't refuse."
—Don Vito Corleone, *The Godfather*

ONE

Drink Like a Mobster!

THERE IS A LITTLE GANGSTER in all of us. And why not! Movies and television programs are filled with stories about the mafia or mobsters. These same shows have made the careers of actors such as Al Pacino, Robert De Niro, Ray Liotta, Joe Pesci, Lorraine Bracco, and Edie Falco, to name a few, while glorifying the mobster lifestyle. The stories that these actors played out on screen tended to always include some of the same elements: the sale of something illegal, the betrayal of someone close, the realization of personal ambitions, and/ or violence either to protect the sale or to avenge a betrayal or as a revenge for a lost family member. When it comes to Mafia movies, art imitates life, because much of what is portrayed on the screen is based on real-life events. Perhaps the allure is that mobsters live on the edge breaking national, state, county, and local laws while at the same time living by an extremely strict code of conduct that includes keeping your mouth shut.

Big-screen blockbusters such as *The Godfather* (1972), *Goodfellas* (1990), and *Scarface* (1983), as well as small-screen hits such as *The Sopranos* (1999–2007), *Boardwalk Empire* (2010–2014), and *The Untouchables* (1959–1963) prove that the

American public has long enjoyed watching Mafia stories. Who can forget the great lines these shows have added to American popular culture?

> "As far back as I can remember, I always wanted to be a gangster." —Henry Hill, *Goodfellas*

> "I'm gonna make him an offer he can't refuse." —Don Vito Corleone, *The Godfather*

> "Leave the gun. Take the cannoli." —Clemenze, *The Godfather*

> "Somebody messes with me, I'm gonna mess with him." —Al Capone, *The Untouchables*

> "Made it, Ma! Top of the World!" —Cody Jarrett, *White Heat*

> "You want to play rough? OK! Say hello to my little friend!" —Tony Montana, *Scarface*

This tough talk followed by action makes life in the Mafia even more appealing. Just think about being able to back up your words with action. The real-life unspeakable violence surrounding illegal liquor and cocktails is firmly rooted in a counterculture reacting to what was seen as intrusive government policy and religious fervor, namely, (1) taxing the production and sale of alcohol—the first tax on the American people by the US Congress—which really amounted to an income tax for the people producing alcohol, including many farmers, but not a tax on all people, and (2) the eventual banning of the production, sale, and transportation of alcohol, which resulted in the period in US history known as Prohibition (1920–1933). Both actions allowed organized crime to move in and fill the void—creating massive unaccountable economic activity based on the sale of illegal unregulated alcoholic beverages. Many of the mobsters ended up spending time in prison after being convicted of evading taxes on their ill-gotten gain. From the perspective of the mob, they were businessmen answering the demand of customers for a scarce product, one that could not be taxed because of alcohol's illicit nature at the time. To use a line from *The Godfather*, "It's not personal; it's strictly business." Of course we learn later, "All business is personal." That is why a mobster had to act to protect his turf or the reason that when mobsters opened speakeasies they were careful to post a set of rules that patrons should follow to remain in the speakeasy.

RULES FOR DRINKING COCKTAILS LIKE A MOBSTER

No credit; pay in advance Cash is always king, but in this case, cash is essential to make sure that the situation does not get messy as a result of trying to collect debts from deadbeats.

Mind the barkeep; his word is law Designating someone to be in charge is always a good business principle.

No sleeping at the tables and no talking politics or religion This rule is just good manners, but not everyone was brought up the same way; sometimes you need to spell it out for people. This rule also prevents a lot of fights and helps to keep order.

In case of raids, down your drink post haste Just get rid of the evidence!

Do not talk in a loud tone; speak easy Enjoy your drink and enjoy your company, but don't draw attention to yourself or the establishment by being too loud.

Secret knocks and passwords will be changed frequently
This is a good customer loyalty program. The more frequently you visit, the more assured you are to have the knock and password changes.

Check all weapons with the doorman This is the best way to make sure that an unpleasant situation does not escalate into a stabbing or a shooting.

No limit on drinks if you can hold your liquor Drink what you want, but don't get crazy!

Any fighting will result in being permanently barred This is a good action/reaction result that is easy to understand.

All drunkards will be harshly dealt with by management If you get crazy, we will beat you down. Again, don't get crazy!

Do not leave the establishment with liquor; remember, this is a dry country The rule speaks for itself . . . and allows everyone to have a little laugh regarding the ironic situation.

The rules were signed at the bottom of the document by the proprietor, who in many cases was a famous mobster—for example, Alphonse (or sometimes "Al") Capone, Charles "Lucky" Luciano, Enoch Lewis "Nucky" Johnson, or simply "Management."

MODERN RULES FOR MAKING COCKTAILS LIKE A MOBSTER

Have at least one or more aliases The best way to avoid having someone pin something on you is to use an alias or two . . . or three. If people must guess who you are, they are less likely to make anything stick.

Have a nickname Adding a nickname adds to your mystique. Thanks to movies and books, almost any nickname will add to your street cred. You might be a CPA (which is a good nickname); you can be "The Accountant" or "The Bookkeeper." If you teach, "The Teacher" or "The Professor." You can use your job, or you can use something about your features. Don't rule anything out.

Know your brands Mobsters know their brands. They know where they come from, and they know what is in the bottles. If you are trying to fence alcohol, you need to know it to sell it. You should also know it when ordering a drink.

Know your drinks You can start off small on this one and learn new ones all the time. An old-fashioned, a Manhattan, a martini, or a gin and tonic will get you started. Learn as many drinks as you can, and be prepared to match a drink to a situation.

Dress for success A real mobster should look good. Men should have a good suit that fits well. Ladies should have a nice dress that fits well. And you need a hat. Hats are a must! What better way to hide your face from the nosy press or the feds?

Call your drinks A real mobster calls the brand that he enjoys. Know what kind of whiskey you want in your Manhattan or what kind of vodka or gin you want in your martini. Mobsters are not afraid to make choices. They are not afraid to ask for what they enjoy drinking.

Pay with cash The easiest way to get in and out of a B & A racket (beer and alcohol racket) is with cash. In addition, bartenders and servers prefer cash, so you can keep them happy, too.

Don't draw attention to yourself Don't lie down if someone challenges you, but try to avoid unneeded attention at all costs. Best to slip in and out of a B & A with little fuss.

Never let a friend drive intoxicated Stand up for your goombata. Never let them drive intoxicated. Best to go to the mattresses and lie low for the evening versus getting pinched by the feds. No one really wants to spend time in the joint.

Don't drive intoxicated Don't get broken.

For those who plan to create their own bar at home or for those who already have a bar, you might consider checking or double-checking to make sure that you have the following items to maximize your and your guests' experience.

MENU

Write a menu of the drinks that you feel confident you can make when your friends visit. Make sure these are drinks that you can produce quickly, with little effort, so that you don't spend time flipping through books. For example, David A. Embury, the author of *The Fine Art of Mixing Cocktails*, which was published in the 1950s, writes that the average host "can get along very nicely" knowing how to make six good cocktails. He suggests the gin martini, the Manhattan, the old-fashioned, the daiquiri, the sidecar, and the Jack Rose, all of which still work almost fourscore years later. Start small and simple with one drink. Once you have perfected the one, set a goal for five drinks, then expand to ten drinks as you learn them, and set the goal of twenty drinks later. Spend time studying drinks away from the bar so that you can expand your menu. A menu will keep you focused and will keep your inventory small and focused, too. The more drinks you add to your menu, the more inventory you will need on hand so that you can produce the drinks on the menu.

SETTING THE BAR

Make sure you have the correct equipment for your bar. You might include one or more of each of the following pieces of equipment. Mobsters are confident and always have the correct tools for the job. They come to the job prepared.

Bar mat Bar mats come in assorted sizes and in assorted colors, which means you can look for the perfect mat to match your bar or the decor of your home. Bar mats provide a stable, slip-free place to mix drinks. Also, bar mats will contain spills and will protect the surface below the mat.

Barspoon The barspoon is one of the most important tools of a bartender. Generally, the barspoon is a very long spoon, about 11 inches, with a twisted handle with a spoon at one end and a disk at the other. The twisted handle aids the bartender in stirring a drink in a mixing glass. The disk can be used to muddle soft items in the bottom of the glass and can be used to layer different alcohols in a glass for a classic layered drink.

Blender Every house and bar should have a blender, no matter what you think of blended drinks. There are some drinks that really should be blended. If you are going to use a blender, make sure to use ice that is already crushed to make sure that you add years to the blades and the overall life of the blender. Examples of blended drinks include the margarita, the piña colada, and daiquiris.

Channel knife A channel knife is a small tool that helps the bartender create citrus twists. The blade of the tool cuts perfect twists both short and long to garnish drinks.

Citrus squeezer Fresh fruit juice makes a cocktail. The citrus squeezer is a tool that comes in numerous sizes specifically for limes, lemons, and other citrus fruits such as oranges and grapefruit. The tool acts as a lever that closes around the fruit, squeezing the juice out of the fruit.

Corkscrew A good corkscrew is important to have on hand to remove corks from bottles and bottle caps. The twisted "worm" is inserted into the cork to grab the cork for removal.

Ice Ice is a tool as well as part of the drink. Ice helps to cool the drink quickly as well as chill the glasses. Ice comes in diverse sizes and shapes. Bartenders should choose the ice size and shape based on the drink being created. Generally, ice comes in three shapes: cubed, crushed, and shaved. Today, there are many choices for molds and cut ice.

Ice scoop Ice should always be scooped into a glass. An ice scoop is a handled scoop that allows the bartender to effortlessly move ice from the ice bin to the mixing glass or to the drinking glass.

Jigger A jigger is a small two-sided hourglass-shaped measuring cup that is used to quickly and accurately measure out various portions of liquor, liqueur, juice, and other liquids to make cocktails. Most common jiggers are 1 ½ ounce on the large side and 1 ounce or less on the small side.

Julep strainer The julep strainer is a curved plate strainer made from stainless steel that is used to strain drinks from the mixing glass when there is no need for a fine strain.

Knife and cutting board A sharp paring knife should always be part of a properly equipped bar. Knifes are used to cut fruit and make garnishes. The cutting board should be small just large enough to hold a piece of fruit.

Muddler A muddler is a small bat-shaped stick of wood or rod of metal. The muddler is used to crush sugar cubes and citrus fruits so they can be incorporated into the drink.

Napkins Napkins add a little class to the drink and will collect any condensation on the outside of the glass so that it does not damage the surface on which the glass is sitting. The color and design of the napkin can coordinate or contrast with the bar.

Pour spout For a professional-looking bar, each bottle should be outfitted with a pour spout. This tool allows the bartender to create a consistent flow of liquid from any bottle. This reliable flow allows the bartender to reduce waste when pouring drinks.

Shaker There are two distinct types of shakers that are used by bartenders: the Boston shaker and the cobbler shaker. The Boston shaker comes in two parts: the tin and the mixing glass. If you use a Boston shaker, you will also need to purchase a strainer to hold the ice in the glass when straining the drink into the glass. The cobbler shaker is a self-contained shaker, tin, and strainer all in one.

Small mesh strainer A small mesh strainer is used to strain out small chips of ice from a drink that is already being strained from a mixing glass or shaker. Sometimes this is referred to as the double strain.

Strainer A drink should always be served over fresh ice, which means a drink that is mixed or shaken should be strained from the mixing glass or the shaker into a glass that contains fresh ice. For a drink that is served straight up, the drink should be strained into a glass that has been chilled with a mixture of ice cubes and water.

Straws Straws are used several ways as tools for bartenders. The straw can be a usable garnish for a drink. The straw gives the drink a finished look and provides guests with a way to sip the drink without touching their lips to the side of the glass. The other use for a straw is for sampling the drink. The bartender can dip the straw into the drink and then put a finger over the top of the straw to create a vacuum that will hold the liquid in the straw. The drink can then be tasted through the open end of the straw. Many bartenders use this technique to make sure that the balance of the drink is correct and to make sure that the drink tastes the way it should taste.

Swizzle sticks Swizzle sticks are used for built drinks, especially drinks from the Caribbean. The swizzle stick is used to mix the drink.

INGREDIENTS

Vodka Vodka is non-aged, clear, distilled spirit with no aroma and no flavor. Vodka can be made from almost anything with sugar. Bartenders like vodka because this neutral spirit sells well and mixes into drinks like a dream.

Gin Gin is a non-aged, clear, distilled spirit with a very distinct flavor and aroma. Gin starts off as a neutral spirit. Each gin is different but most will have juniper berry in the flavor and aroma. Many mixed drinks are made with gin.

Rum Rum is a distilled spirit that can be non-aged or aged. Made from sugarcane, rum is an excellent mixer.

Tequila Tequila is a distilled spirit that can be non-aged or aged. This spirit is made from the agave plant. Unlike all the other spirits that are made from an annual crop, like corn or wheat, tequila's agave takes almost a decade to grow. So great planning goes into tequila's production.

Brandy Brandy is a distilled spirit that can be non-aged or aged. Brandy is made from fruit wine, in most cases grape wine. Many popular brandies are aged in casks that give a golden color to the brandy.

Whiskey Whiskey is a distilled spirit that can be non-aged or aged. Whiskey is made from grain beer. All types of grains are used to make whiskey, although certain whiskeys require specific grains.

Liqueurs A liqueur is a sweetened, flavored spirit that is often used as a mixer, although liqueurs can be consumed by themselves before or after a meal. Flavors vary. Fruits, nuts, and herbs make up most of the liqueurs on the market.

Fortified wine Fortified wine is wine with brandy added to raise the alcohol content. Originally for storage and shipping, the increased alcohol also makes a terrific addition to a cocktail.

Fresh juice Cocktails are better with fresh squeezed juice. Most cocktails that feature juice contain a citrus juice: lime, lemon, orange, or grapefruit. Make sure to have enough to make cocktails for your party. Make sure that cocktails with juice are shaken.

Garnishes Most cocktails have prescriptive garnishes. For example, the Tom Collins always comes with an orange slice and a cocktail cherry, which is the same garnish for the old-fashioned. The Manhattan is garnished with a cocktail cherry, and the horse's neck comes with a long lemon twist. Make sure to know the proper garnishes and have plenty of garnishes for your party.

Some of the recipes you will make will call for simple syrup, which is simple and cheap to make. Some recipes call for sugar and water, but simple syrup will save time and will ensure that the sugar is completely dissolved. Here is a recipe for a good simple syrup to make at home.

OMEMADE SIMPLE SYRUP

Yield: about 2 cups
1 cup water
1 ½ cup sugar

Place both the water and the sugar into a small pot.
Bring the mixture to a boil for three minutes, then
take the resulting syrup off the heat and let cool.
Put the syrup into a plastic bottle and use as needed.

Anytime a drink calls for lime or lemon juice and simple syrup, you can substitute sour mix. For example, if the drink calls for 1 ounce of lemon juice and ½ ounce simple syrup, then 1 ½ ounces of sour mix can be used instead. The following is a good sour mix to use at a home bar and builds on the knowledge of making simple syrup.

OMEMADE SOUR MIX

1 ½ cup sugar
1 cup water
1 cup fresh squeezed lemon juice

½ cup fresh squeezed lime juice
½ cup fresh squeezed orange juice

*Start by squeezing enough lemons, limes, and oranges
to have the needed quantity of juice. Mix the juice
and refrigerate. Make the simple syrup with the
sugar and the water by boiling for 3 minutes. Cool the
simple syrup, then add to the fresh squeezed juice.*

Grenadine is a sweet and tart syrup used to flavor and color
drinks a shade of red or pink. The origin of the word *grenadine*
comes from the French word *grenade*, which means *pomegranate*. This is an easy recipe to make and will elevate drinks
beyond the store-bought version.

OMEMADE GRENADINE

Yield: 2 cups
1 cup pomegranate juice (no sugar added)
1 ½ cup sugar
½ teaspoon fresh squeezed lemon juice

*Pour the sugar and pomegranate juice into a pot.
Warm, stirring the whole time until the sugar
dissolves into the juice. Pull from heat and allow to
cool. Once cool, add the lemon juice. Store in bottles
or jars under refrigeration. Use as needed.*

There are some very good cocktail cherries on the market. If cherries are in season, you might try making them yourself. Here is an easy recipe that will get you started.

HOMEMADE COCKTAIL CHERRIES

40 fresh cherries
¼ teaspoon cinnamon
2 cups plus ¼ cup bourbon (or your favorite spirit)

Pit the cherries. Heat a pan on the stove, and pour the cherries into the pan and sauté in the ¼ cup bourbon. If the cherries catch the flame, remove from the stove until the flame burns out. Add the cinnamon and mix. Pour the cherries into a sanitized jar and cover with bourbon. Allow to cool and refrigerate. Serve with your favorite cocktail that calls for a cocktail cherry.

GLASSWARE

Champagne flute A champagne flute is a tall drink glass designed to hold sparkling wine. With a narrow opening at the top, the glass effectively holds the CO_2 and releases the gas slowly, allowing for tiny streams of bubbles to float to the top of the glass. This glass is great for many cocktails including the Seelbach cocktail and the French 75.

Cocktail glass Also known as a martini glass, this is the perfect vessel for a chilled drink served straight-up. The V-shaped glass is iconic.

Highball glass Perfect for long drinks, this tall glass holds ice as well as at least 10 ounces of liquid.

Hurricane glass An hourglass-shaped glass used for the hurricane cocktail and other drinks.

Margarita glass A glass specifically for the margarita with a large flat bowl at the top.

Mug A large vessel used for beer and cocktails.

Mule mug This distinctive copper mug is traditionally used for the mule family of drinks.

Old-fashioned A glass with straight sides and a flat bottom. Also known as a low-ball glass or a rocks glass.

Pilsner glass Perfect for a glass of beer or for a beer cocktail.

Pint glass Used for beer and cocktails.

Red wine glass A wineglass with a large bowl on top and a long stem.

Shot glass A small glass that holds between 1 and 2 ounces or a shot of spirits.

White wine glass A wineglass with a small bowl on top and a long stem.

Bartenders use several techniques to make drinks properly. Each drink calls for a specific technique. Knowing how to make drinks using these techniques will increase street credibility for the home bartender.

TECHNIQUES

Blending Using the blending technique is important for drinks such as the blended margarita, daiquiri, or piña colada. Blending is important for incorporating thick dairy products and whole or frozen fruit. Try to use less ice because too much ice will water down the finished drink. A happy medium is to use some ice and frozen fruit to maximize the flavor of the drink. Crushed ice should always be used for this technique to help extend the life and blades of the blender. When using crushed ice, be sure to blend for 20 seconds, stop, then blend for 10 seconds.

Building Building a drink is simply pouring one ingredient into the glass after another until all the ingredients are in the glass. This technique is used for gin and tonics, Moscow mules, Collinses, and screwdrivers.

Layering The layering technique involves the bartender's knowledge of the specific gravity of a liquid. The heavier liquids are used as a base while the lighter liquids are floated (or layered) on top of the heavier liquids to create a layered appearance in the glass. Examples of layered drinks include the B-52, the tequila sunrise, the black and tan, and the classic pousse-café.

Muddling The technique of muddling is highlighted by the bartender's use of a muddler to crush sugar, citrus fruit, or herbs before adding ice and alcohol to the drink. Generally, the herb or fruit should be lightly muddled so as not to release bitter flavors of overmuddled items. The old-fashioned, caipirinha, mint julep, and mojito are examples of muddled drinks.

Shaking The shaking method is used for drinks that need to combine ingredients that might not easily combine in a uniform manner any other way. Shaking will also aerate the cocktail, allowing for a foam or froth on top of the cocktail. Cocktails with citrus juice or egg whites are typically shaken cocktails. Examples of cocktails that use the shaking method are the cosmopolitan, the kamikaze, and the sidecar.

Stirring Stirring is perfect for drinks that are completely made from alcoholic beverage. The purpose of stirring the drink is to make sure that you have a result that is crystal clear. To complete this technique, fill a mixing glass with ice, then pour the ingredients into the glass. Using a barspoon, stir the drink at least forty turns or until completely chilled. Top the mixing glass with a strainer and pour the drink into a chilled glass or a glass with ice. The Manhattan, negroni, and martini are examples of stirred cocktails.

COCKTAIL CREATION: A BALANCING ACT

Keep in mind that cocktail creation is a balancing act. A great cocktail is not too sweet, not too sour, and not too bitter. The perfect cocktail is *just right*. When you see a bartender stick a straw into a drink to syphon out a sip of a cocktail, the bartender is checking for balance in flavor.

A great cocktail to play with on this point is the old-fashioned. The home bartender can play around with the recipe to see how each of the elements plays a part in the overall cocktail. In the case of the old-fashioned, the sugar melts into the water and provides the sweet element of the cocktail. Bitters is added to help elevate the flavor of the cocktail and to counter the sweet so that the sweet is not too sweet. The spirit is added and brings the cocktail together. But wait, what type of spirit? Each spirit will have a different reaction to the overall recipe. The old-fashioned will have a different balance and different flavor based on the spirit.

Another cocktail that the home bartender can play around with is the homemade margarita. This is a splendid example of a "sour" drink. We want the margarita to be sour but not too sour, which is why we balance the drink with sweet. Again, we don't want this drink to be too sweet. This balance in flavor is important.

"As far back as I can remember, I always wanted to be a gangster." —Henry Hill, *Goodfellas*

TWO

People, Places, and Things

BOOTLEGGING

Bootlegging is the illegal practice of transporting alcoholic beverages where that transportation is prohibited by law. The term probably dates back to the Civil War when soldiers sneaked alcohol into camps by placing the alcohol into flasks and hiding the flasks in their boots. During Prohibition, drivers took cars with two gas tanks across the Ambassador Bridge in Detroit, filled up one tank (not connected to the engine) with whiskey in Windsor, Canada, and drove back to the Motor City. The term has now expanded to include any item that is illegal.

SPEAKEASY

Speakeasies are illegal bars. The term and concept predates Prohibition, but speakeasies exist today. The original purpose of a speakeasy was for the owners of such place to avoid paying tax on the sale of alcohol. During Prohibition, the concept took on a new purpose; to sell and serve alcohol illegally. The name *speakeasy* comes from the words *speak* and *easy*, which is how a patron was to approach and speak a password through the door to gain access. The term *speakeasy* is interchangeable with *blind pig* and *blind tiger*. Speakeasy establishments exploded during Prohibition.

THE FIVE POINTS GANG

The Five Points Gang was a gangster incubator in the late nineteenth and early twentieth century. The gang was founded by Paolo Antonio Vaccarelli, a.k.a. Paul Kelly. Some of the gang's famous alumni include young Charles "Lucky" Luciano, Al "Scarface" Capone, Capone's mentor Johnny "The Fox" Torrio, Meyer Lansky, and Benjamin "Bugsy" Siegel, to name a few, who all graduated on to infamous mobster careers spanning the United States and beyond. The gang was named for a section of lower Manhattan known as Five Points near the Manhattan and Brooklyn Bridges.

EIGHTEENTH AMENDMENT (VOLSTEAD ACT)

The Eighteenth Amendment of the US Constitution was proposed by the US Senate on August 1, 1917, in a bipartisan vote with thirty-six Democrats and twenty-nine Republicans voting in favor of the resolution. The House of Representatives with 141 Democrats, 137 Republicans, and 4 Independents voted in favor of a revised resolution on December 17, 1917, which was approved by the Senate the next day on December 18, 1917. This action formally approved the proposed change by Congress to the states. Mississippi's state legislature was the first to ratify the change on January 7, 1918, followed by the state legislatures, in order, of Virginia, Kentucky, North Dakota, South Carolina, Maryland, Montana, Texas, Delaware, South Dakota, Massachusetts, Arizona, Georgia, Louisiana, and Florida by the end of 1918. Michigan's legislature continued the effort in 1919, followed by Ohio, Oklahoma, Idaho, Maine, West Virginia, California, Tennessee, Washington, Arkansas, Illinois, Indiana, Kansas, Alabama, Colorado, Iowa, New Hampshire, Oregon, North Carolina, Utah, Nebraska (January 16, 1919, which allowed the Amendment to be added to the Constitution), Missouri, Wyoming, Minnesota, Wisconsin, New Mexico, Nevada, New York, Vermont, Pennsylvania, and New Jersey (New Jersey ratified on March 9, 1922, more than two years after the Eighteenth Amendment was already in effect over the whole United States). Connecticut and Rhode Island never ratified the Amendment.

The text of the Eighteenth Amendment reads as follows:

Section 1. After one year from the ratification of this article the manufacture, sale, or transportation of intoxicating liquors within, the importation thereof into, or the exportation thereof from the United States and all the territory subject to the jurisdiction thereof for beverage purposes is hereby prohibited.

Section 2. The Congress and the several States shall have concurrent power to enforce this article by appropriate legislation.

Section 3. This article shall be inoperative unless it shall have been ratified as an amendment to the Constitution by the legislatures of the several States, as provided in the Constitution, within seven years from the date of the submission hereof to the States by the Congress.

Please note that the Amendment did not take effect until one year after ratification on January 19, 1920, and the Amendment never limited consumption of alcohol. Cutting off the supply but not addressing the demand opened the door for organized crime to fill the void. The Eighteenth Amendment remains the only Amendment to the US Constitution that (1) limits a freedom of citizens and (2) was repealed by another Amendment to the Constitution (Twenty-First Amendment).

BATHTUB GIN

Bathtub gin is an illicit spirit made by mixing a neutral spirit with juniper berry oil; it was very popular during Prohibition. Many times, it was made in the bathroom because of the air gap between the faucet and the drink in the bathtub, which allows bottles to fit underneath the faucet to cut the alcohol with water and/or the alcohol can be mixed in the bathtub. The bathroom also provided the seclusion necessary to mix this spirit during Prohibition.

RUM-RUNNING

Rum-running is the practice of illegally importing spirit into the United States during Prohibition. Many times rum-running originated in the Bahamas or the Caribbean and was not limited to rum. The rumrunner (someone who participated in rum-running) often transported the spirit just short of US waters where the spirit was transferred to another ship that took it the rest of the way.

MOONSHINE

Moonshine is an illegal spirit made without government approval and without tax from the federal government. The term *moonshine* dates back to eighteenth-century England, when illicit spirit was moved to the coastline on ships. Moonshine also describes the time of day the spirit was made—that is, at night, when the smoke of the stills could not be seen by government agents. Moonshine is also known as shine and white lightning. In recent years, several legal labels of shine have made their way to liquor store shelves.

OWNEY VINCENT MADDEN, A.K.A. THE KILLER

Owney Madden was born in England. After immigrating to the United States as a child, he started as a member of the Gopher Gang in New York's Hell's Kitchen. By his eighteenth birthday, he was the suspect in the deaths of five rival gang members. Several years later, the tables turned as members of the Hudson Dusters shot Madden eleven times. Incredibly, he survived, but five of the bullets remained in him for the rest of his life. Madden later killed some members of the Dusters; he served time in Sing-Sing Prison for one of those murders. After more than eight years, Madden was released in 1923, when he began importing all types of distilled spirits into the United States during Prohibition. Also, Madden owned the famous Cotton Club and was a promoter for many boxers including World Heavyweight Champion Primo Carnera. In 1935, Madden left Manhattan and relocated to Hot Springs, Arkansas, where he lived for the rest of his life. He opened the Southern Club which was a popular destination for mobsters; in fact, Lucky Luciano was apprehended there in 1935. Madden became a US citizen in 1943 and died in 1965 of natural causes.

ALPHONSE "AL" GABRIEL CAPONE, A.K.A. SCARFACE

Al Capone was one of nine children and grew up in Brooklyn. He quickly rose through the ranks of organized crime, starting with the Five Points Gang in New York and graduating to the right-hand man of Johnny Torrio in Chicago. When Torrio retired from the Chicago Outfit, then twenty-six-year-old Capone took over and expanded the family business in the Second City organization. Their reputation was second to none. During his seven year reign as a mob boss, he enjoyed many designations, ranging from "modern-day Robin Hood" to "public enemy number one." Eventually, he was tried and convicted for tax evasion, ending his mob career and starting a prison sentence that lasted longer than his term as mob boss. He died in Florida at the age of forty-eight from complications of neurosyphilis. Several of Capone's brothers figured into Prohibition: Raffaele James Capone, a.k.a. Ralph "Bottles" Capone and public enemy number three, ran his younger brother's bottling operation in Chicago. Their eldest brother, James Vinvenzo Capone, changed his name to Richard James Hart after moving to Nebraska from Brooklyn. Hart served the United States in World War I and later as a Prohibition agent.

ADELARD CUNIN,
A.K.A. GEORGE "BUGS" MORAN

Chicago was not only ruled by Al "Scarface" Capone, but Bugs Moran also ran another family, the North Side Gang. The rival organizations battled each other for control of the Windy City. Moran escaped death in the Saint Valentine's Day Massacre because he slept in on February 14, 1929. Moran, a Minnesota native, died in February 1957 in Leavenworth Prison of lung cancer.

SAINT VALENTINE'S DAY MASSACRE

On February 14, 1929, at 10:30 a.m., more than seventy shots from two Thompson submachine guns and two shotguns mowed down seven men at a warehouse at 2122 North Clark Street in Chicago. The crime was never solved, although there are many theories about it. Undisputed is that of the seven victims, five were members of George "Bugs" Moran's North Side Gang, including Albert Kachellek, Adam Heyer, Albert

Weinshank, and the two Gusenberg brothers (see below), and the other two were associates of the gang, including John May and Reinhardt Schwimmer. Of the four perpetrators, some were dressed as Chicago policemen.

FRANK GUSENBERG

Frank Gusenberg was the last surviving victim of the Saint Valentine's Day Massacre and brother to Peter "Goosey" Gusenberg, who was also a victim on February 14, 1929. The Gusenberg brothers were known associates of George "Bugs" Moran. Frank was shot more than seven times but was still alive when the police arrived. When asked by the Chicago police, "Who shot you?" Frank responded, "Nobody shot me."

FRANK COSTELLO, A.K.A. THE PRIME MINISTER

Frank Costello was one of the most powerful, influential, and long-lived mobsters. In the 1920s, he helped to run bootlegging and rum-running operations in New York. During that time, he was indicted on federal charges but was not convicted because the jury ended in a deadlock. Costello was considered an important link between the mob and Tammany Hall politicians. Born in Italy, Costello served as the consigliere of the Luciano crime family—later the Genovese crime family—until Lucky Luciano was sentenced to prison and underboss Vito Genovese, indicted on murder, left the United States for Italy. Costello served as a very popular boss of the family for twenty years but stepped down after an assassination attempt in 1957. Genovese regained control of the family upon Costello's retirement.

ENOCH LEWIS "NUCKY" JOHNSON

Nucky was a good guy gone bad—impeccably dressed with a red carnation in his lapel. He ruled Atlantic City for more than 30 years through the legitimate political process. Johnson served first as Atlantic County sheriff and then as Atlantic County treasurer. He was involved in bootlegging among other crimes. Johnson was a member of the Combined or the Big Seven Group, where he partnered with Johnny Torrio, Lucky Luciano, and Meyer Lansky, among others. Johnson was convicted of tax evasion in 1941. He served in prison until 1945 and died of natural causes in 1968. Actor Steve Buscemi portrayed a fictionalized version of Johnson as Nucky Thompson in HBO's *Boardwalk Empire*.

CHARLES "LUCKY" LUCIANO

Lucky was an organized crime visionary. He was the founding boss of what became the Genovese crime family. Luciano is credited with helping to end the Castellammarese War between Joe "The Boss" Masseria and Salvatore Maranzano and with founding the Commission. In 1936, Luciano was sentenced to thirty to fifty years in state prison on sixty-two counts of compulsory prostitution. At first, he tried to continue to run the family from prison, but when the US Supreme Court refused to hear his appeal, he relinquished control of the family to Frank Costello. In 1946, Luciano was released from prison in exchange for his assistance to the United States during World War II. He was immediately deported to Italy but secretly moved to Havana, Cuba, six months later. Later that year, he attended a December meeting, known as the Havana Conference, of all of the crime families, which blew his cover. The United States asked Cuba to expel Luciano back to Italy, where he was closely monitored until his death in 1962. He was portrayed by Christian Slater in the 1991 film *Mobsters*, which lays out a semifictional account of the creation of the Commission.

THE BIG SEVEN, A.K.A. THE COMBINED

The Combined was an East Coast criminal organization in the 1920s during the height of Prohibition. Membership included representation from New York, New Jersey, Ohio, Pennsylvania, and Rhode Island, to name a few and included the who's who of the East Coast organized crime. The Combined was the cornerstone of the 1929 Atlantic City Conference and the forerunner of the National Crime Syndicate.

THE FIVE FAMILIES, A.K.A. THE COMMISSION

The Commission replaced the dictatorial boss of all bosses (capo di tutti capi) with a democratic representative governing body for the Mafia in the United States. The Commission was conceived by Lucky Luciano at the end of the Castellammarese War. Founded in 1931, the Commission consists of at least twenty-one families, but only six have seats on the Commission including the Bonanno family, the Chicago Outfit, the Colombo family, the Gambino family, the Genovese family, and the Lucchese family. The Genovese family represents the interests of the crime families from Buffalo, Cleveland, Detroit, New England (Patriarca family), New Jersey (the DeCavalcante family), New Orleans, Philadelphia, and Pittsburgh. The Chicago Outfit represents the interests of the crime families from Kansas City, Los Angeles, Milwaukee, San Francisco, San Jose, Saint Louis, and Tampa (the Trafficante family).

DUTCH SCHULTZ

Never disobey the Commission! Had Dutch Schultz remembered this, he might have lived beyond age thirty-three. Schultz was born Arthur Simon Flegenheimer in 1902 and was the son of German-Jewish immigrants in New York City. Schultz became wealthy during Prohibition in part thanks to bootlegging and rum-running. Enter Thomas Dewey, who was at the time a US district attorney. Dewey decided to take Schultz down. Eventually, Dewey ran for president of the United States. He did not defeat Franklin D. Roosevelt in 1944 nor did he defeat Harry S. Truman in 1948, but he did defeat Schultz. Schultz wanted to eliminate Dewey, so he asked permission to kill the attorney. The Commission denied the request. Schultz decided to go ahead with the murder, but the Commission heard about the plan and had Schultz killed before he could bring the plan to fruition. Schultz, who had converted to Roman Catholicism in the years before he was killed, was administered last rites by a priest before he died and is buried in the Gates of Heaven Cemetery in Hawthorne, New York.

MAFIA RANKS AND STRUCTURE

Boss The boss is the head of a crime family. The boss is the one who give the orders for the family to follow or is the chief executive officer of the family.

Underboss The underboss is second only to the boss.

Consigliere The consigliere gives advice to the boss.

Capo A capo or captain is the street commander.

Soldier (made man) The soldier is an accepted member of the family. Soldiers are also known as made men. To become a made man, an associate is recommended or endorsed by two crime family members, has either (1) committed two murders or (2) brings great financial gain to the family, and must be genetically acceptable. For example, someone of Irish decent might be an associate of the Italian Mafia but will never be a full member because of his Irish decent.

Associate An associate works for a family but is not a full member of the family.

OMERTÀ

Omertà is the code of silence that each member of the Mafia must follow. Breaking this code is punishable by death.

THE PURPLE GANG

Prohibition came early to Michigan with passage of the Damon Act of 1917. Detroit had one of the most ruthless gang of bootleggers in the country, the Purple Gang. The gang was headed by native New Yorker brothers Abe, Izzy, Joe, and Raymond Bernstein, who relocated to Detroit. The quartet led a group that was so evil that they were "rotten, purple like the color of bad meat." In fact, Al Capone did not expand to Detroit in order to avoid battling the Bernsteins and their Purple Gang.

THE REAL MCCOY

Teetotaler Captain William "Bill" McCoy and his brother Ben were rumrunners during Prohibition. When the McCoys fell on hard times during Prohibition, they turned to rum-running. They sailed to the Bahamas, then back to the United States. They anchored in international waters where they transferred the cargo to smaller ships. The brothers delivered unmolested product to their customers. The US Coast Guard finally caught Captain McCoy and shut down the family business. The idiom *the real McCoy* predates Captain McCoy, but people during Prohibition indicated that the spirits were "the real McCoy" as mark of quality.

NASCAR

The National Association for Stock Car Auto Racing (NASCAR) traces its genesis to Prohibition when bootleggers and rumrunners modified their cars to carry more cargo but still run faster as a way to avoid the feds. Some of the locations, such as Daytona Beach, where cars race today, have their roots in Prohibition.

TWENTY-FIRST AMENDMENT

The Twenty-First Amendment to the US Constitution is the only Constitutional Amendment that repeals another Amendment to the Constitution, in this case the Eighteenth Amendment. The Twenty-First Amendment is unique for another reason: it is the only Amendment that directly creates industry—the production, sale, and transportation of alcohol.

CARLO "THE GODFATHER" GAMBINO

Carlo was born in Sicily to a family involved with the Sicilian Mafia. He earned his button by the age of nineteen. Carlo was known for being low key and discreet. He immigrated to the United States in 1921, where he became the boss of the Gambino family and then the chairman of the Commission. He was the brother-in-law and cousin of Paul "Big Paul" Castellano. He beat charges on tax evasion and later died of a heart attack at the age of seventy-four in 1976. Castellano succeeded him as the boss of the Gambino family and chairman of the Commission. His nickname may have been used by Mario Puzo for his novel *The Godfather*.

"You want to play rough? OK! Say hello to my little friend!"
—Tony Montana, *Scarface*

THREE

Recipes

EVERY ALCOHOLIC BEVERAGE IS FERMENTED. Fermented beverages such as beer and wine can be served, but they can also be distilled into a spirit at a higher alcohol by volume. Spirits fall into three categories: (1) clear spirits, (2) brown spirits, and (3) spirits that are sometimes clear and sometimes brown. All of these spirit categories are represented in this chapter. First, the clear spirits, vodka and gin; then the spirits that come both clear and brown, rum and tequila (and mescal); followed by the brown spirits, brandy and whiskey; and finally, other cocktails that are made with wine, beer, or liqueurs.

VODKA

Vodka is a favorite spirit among bartenders because it is colorless, flavorless, and has little aroma (in other words, is neutral) once it is mixed into a cocktail; these characteristics allow maximum creativity from the bartender. Vodka's indistinguishable character is achieved by distilling the spirit to a higher alcohol by volume and then watering it back down to the desired proof. Smirnoff capitalized on this in 1953, creating an ad campaign, "It leaves you breathless," which was a play on words. The vodka was undetectable when mixed with other beverages such as orange juice, tomato juice, or tonic water. Most other spirits can be detected on the breath of the person consuming that spirit. Vodka can be made from anything, but most are made from grains or potatoes. Today, vodka is one of the most popular spirits with bar customers. Due to vodka's flavor profile and popularity with customers, the Mafia easily produced and sold it during Prohibition.

VODKA COCKTAILS

During Prohibition, many fishing boats traveled around Cape Cod trying to catch fish. Dressing up as fishing crews was a terrific way for mobsters and rumrunners to hide in plain sight. The Cape Cod area is also known for its cranberry bogs and the production of cranberries. This recipe combines both. You might try trading out the vodka for rum.

APE CODDER

1 ½ ounces vodka
3 ounces cranberry juice
½ ounce fresh squeezed lime juice
Lime wedge

Fill an old-fashioned glass with ice. Add the vodka, lime juice, and cranberry juice. Garnish with a lime wedge and serve.

A Bay Breeze is similar to a Cape Codder. This cocktail is distinct because of the addition of grapefruit juice and the use of the highball glass.

AY BREEZE

2 ounces vodka
2 ounces pink grapefruit juice
4 ounces cranberry juice
Lime wedge
Ice

Fill a highball glass with ice. Pour the vodka into the glass, followed by grapefruit juice and then cranberry juice. Garnish with a wedge of lime. Serve.

The long blade of the machete can be used to strike fear into someone or to hurt someone. As a weapon, the machete can be used in a comparable way to an ax or a short sword with maximum damage. This cocktail combines vodka with pineapple juice and tonic water for a well-balanced drink. Be careful of the edge of the machete!

ACHETE

1 ounce vodka
2 ounces pineapple juice
3 ounces tonic water
Ice

Fill a double old-fashioned glass with ice. To a mixing glass add ice, vodka, pineapple juice, and tonic water. Stir. Then strain the drink into the chilled glass.

The Gimlet would have been known to mobsters before and during Prohibition. One of the most difficult drinks to make is the Vodka Gimlet. There should be a balance between the vodka and the lime. Too much lime and the drink will be too tart, whereas not enough will make the drink too strong.

GIMLET

1 ½ ounces vodka
½ ounce Rose's sweetened lime juice
Thin slice of lime
Ice

Fill a cocktail glass with ice and water to chill. Fill the tin side of a Boston shaker with ice. Add the vodka and Rose's sweetened lime juice into the glass side of the shaker, then pour the liquid into the tin and attach the two sides. Shake until the combination is cold. Discard the ice and water in the cocktail glass. Strain the Gimlet into the cocktail glass, then float the lime on top. Serve.

A drink that is like the Gimlet in ingredients is the Kamikaze. While Al Capone and his contemporaries might not have seen this cocktail, there would have been high demand for this drink at speakeasies. This was the go-to drink at Cliff's Lounge in Lincoln, Nebraska, when I was studying at the University of Nebraska–Lincoln.

AMIKAZE

2 ounces vodka
1 ounce fresh lime juice
1 ounce triple sec

Prepare two shot glasses. Add ice to the tin side of a Boston shaker. Add vodka, lime juice, and triple sec to the glass side of the shaker. Pour the liquid into the tin side and attach the two sides. Shake the Boston shaker until the beverage is cold, then strain equally into the waiting shot glasses. Enjoy!

The 1994 film *Pulp Fiction* was a landmark movie. Quentin Tarantino scored an Oscar for Best Original Screenplay, and John Travolta earned an Oscar nomination for Best Actor for playing Vincent Vega. In the opening scene, Vega and partner in crime Jules Winnfield, played by Samuel L. Jackson (nominated for Best Supporting Actor), discuss foot massages. During the discussion, they talk about how an acquaintance, Tony "Rocky Horror," was thrown from the fourth story of a building for giving the boss's wife a foot massage and "developed a speech impediment." Winnfield says, "That shit ain't right. . . . [If he does that to me] he better paralyze my ass cuz I kill him."

PARALYZER

1 ounce vodka
1 ounce coffee liqueur
2 ounces milk or cream
4 ounces cola
Ice
Cocktail cherry

Add ice to a highball glass. Then add vodka, coffee-flavored liqueur, and then cola. Stir gently. Add the milk or cream to the top, then garnish with a cocktail cherry. Serve.

The screwdriver is a perfect mobster drink. During Prohibition, alcoholic drinks needed to be out of plain sight. Therefore, what better ingredients to use than wholesome orange juice and colorless and flavorless vodka.

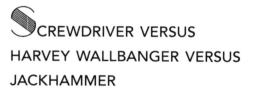

SCREWDRIVER VERSUS HARVEY WALLBANGER VERSUS JACKHAMMER

1 ½ ounces vodka
6 ounces orange juice
Ice
Orange slice

Fill a highball glass with ice. Add vodka and then orange juice. Stir. Add the orange slice to the rim and serve.
If you want to make this a Harvey Wallbanger, add ½ ounce of Galliano to the drink after the vodka and before the orange juice. If you would like to try a Jackhammer, substitute pineapple juice for the orange juice.

The races seem like a natural place for mobsters to hang out. They run the races, they run the numbers, and/or they loan money to people to "play the ponies" or bet at the greyhound track. The greyhound is like the screwdriver but uses grapefruit juice instead of orange juice. Add salt to the rim of the glass for a salty dog. You can also substitute gin for the vodka. Tequila transforms the drink into a Chihuahua.

REYHOUND (SALTY DOG)

1 ½ ounces vodka
6 ounces grapefruit juice
Ice
Orange slice

Fill a highball glass with ice. Add the vodka, then the orange juice. Stir. Add the orange slice to the rim and serve.

When you don't know the name of the drink but it looks good, just point and ask for one of those . . . or in this case, One of Those, which is like a cosmopolitan but with amaretto instead of triple sec.

NE OF THOSE

1 ½ ounces vodka
6 ounces cranberry juice
½ ounce amaretto
½ ounce lime juice

Add ice and water to a highball glass to chill the glass. Add ice to the tin side of a Boston shaker. In the mixing glass, add vodka, cranberry juice, amaretto, and lime juice. Pour the contents of the mixing glass into the iced tin and secure the glass to the tin. Shake the contents until the ice sounds different and the contents are cold. Open the Boston shaker. Empty the highball glass, add new ice, and strain the contents of the shaker into the empty glass. Serve.

Agent Orange borrows the name from a defoliant used by the US military during the Vietnam War. There is a small turf war over the Agent Orange cocktail. There are two very different drinks made with this name. One focuses on the color of the cocktail, whereas the other focuses on the flavor. Try both and make your decision.

GENT ORANGE #1

1 ½ ounces vodka
5 ounces carrot juice

Fill an old-fashioned glass with ice.
Add vodka, then carrot juice. Stir and serve.

GENT ORANGE #2

1 ounce vodka
1 ounce Cointreau
2 ounces fresh squeezed orange juice
Orange twist

Add ice and water to a cocktail glass to chill the glass.
Add ice to the tin side of a Boston shaker. In the mixing glass,
add vodka, Cointreau, and orange juice. Pour the contents
of the mixing glass into the iced tin and secure the glass to
the tin. Shake the contents until the ice sounds different
and the contents are cold. Open the Boston shaker. Empty
the cocktail glass, then strain the contents of the shaker
into the empty glass. Squeeze the orange twist over the
drink, and rub the twist around the rim of the glass. Serve.

The 1983 movie *Scarface* features perhaps one of the most iconic lines from any gangster movie. The movie's screenplay, written by Oliver Stone, tells the story of Tony Montana, played by Al Pacino. Toward the end of the movie, Montana yells, "You want to play rough! OK! Say hello to my little friend!" Montana then pulls the trigger on a grenade launcher. The explosion disables the first wave of attackers trying to kill him. Montana then shoots the attackers to make sure that each is dead. This cocktail, which is served in a shot glass, memorializes that line.

AY HELLO TO MY LITTLE FRIEND

1 ounce vodka
½ ounce rye
½ ounce triple sec

Fill the tin part of a Boston shaker with ice. In the glass part, pour vodka, rye, and triple sec. Shake until cold and strain into a shot glass. Serve.

Feeling like a gangster? Make a gangster martini. The combination of vodka, nutty and orange liqueurs, and pineapple juice makes for a tasty combination. The original recipe used Brown-Forman products and featured a cocktail cherry for garnish. However, have as many cherries as you would like. After all, you are a gangster.

ANGSTER MARTINI

1 ½ ounces pineapple juice
1 ounce Tuaca
1 ounce amaretto
1 ounce vodka
Cocktail cherries

Fill a cocktail glass with ice and water to chill the glass. Then fill the tin side of a Boston shaker with ice. Measure out the pineapple juice, Tuaca, amaretto, and vodka into the glass side of the shaker. Pour the mixture into the tin and close the shaker. Shake until the ice sounds different. Empty the cocktail glass and strain the cocktail into the glass. Serve.

GIN

Gin begins as a neutral spirit (like vodka), but the spirit is exposed to a brand-specific proprietary mixture of seeds, roots, barks, herbs, and spices, with the most common being juniper berries. During Prohibition, many people, including the Mafia, made a similar tasting product, "bathtub gin," by taking a neutral spirit and adding oils or extracts of juniper berries to arrive at the desired flavor. Some gin cocktails exist because of the bathtub gin era when mixing something with the gin helped to cover the bad flavors of the bathtub gin. Many excellent cocktails rely on gin's specific flavor.

GIN COCKTAILS

For a verbal time warp to a hundred years in the past, consider ordering a "bee's knees." In the 1920s, the phrase meant "excellent" or "the highest quality." This cocktail is like the lemon drop martini except for the use of gin and the honey simple syrup. The combination is a wonderful palate cleanser and very good for the beginning of a meal.

 EE'S KNEES

½ ounce of fresh squeezed lemon juice
½ ounce honey simple syrup
2 ounces gin
Lemon twist or thin lemon slice

Add ice and water into a cocktail glass to chill the glass. Add ice to a cocktail shaker or to the tin side of a Boston shaker. Add lemon juice, honey syrup, and then gin to the mixing glass. Pour the contents of the mixing glass into the tin and make sure the two sides are attached tightly. Shake until you hear the ice change in sound. Open the Boston shaker and pull the mixing glass side off. Empty the cocktail glass and strain the drink into the chilled cocktail glass. Garnish with a lemon twist or a lemon slice.

Bijou is the French word for "jewel." Equal parts of gin, vermouth, and Chartreuse with a dash of orange bitters ensure that this cocktail is no fugazi—like the cocktail listed in *The Old Waldorf-Astoria Bar Book* with the same name. The bijou cocktail has an impressive pedigree as the brainchild of

Harry Johnson and featured in his classic text, *Harry Johnson's 1882 New and Improved Bartenders' Manual and a Guide for Hotels and Restaurants.* In his recipe, Johnson recommends Plymouth gin and suggests either a cherry or a medium-sized olive and a lemon twist. The bijou would have been a familiar drink to bartenders, patrons, and their mobster hosts before, during, and after Prohibition.

BIJOU

1 dash of orange bitters
1 ounce Plymouth gin
1 ounce sweet vermouth
1 ounce green Chartreuse
Cocktail cherry
Lemon twist

Add ice to a cocktail glass and a little water to chill the glass, then set the glass aside. Add ice to the mixing glass. Start with the dash of orange bitters. Add gin, vermouth, and Chartreuse. Stir until chilled (about forty stirs). Empty the cocktail glass. Add cocktail cherry to the bottom of the cocktail glass. Strain the mixed bijou from the mixing glass into the cocktail glass. Twist the lemon twist over the drink to express the lemon oils over the glass and then rub the rim of the glass with the twist. Add the twist to the drink and serve.

New York City has the five boroughs as well as the Five Families, which may just be a coincidence because each family conducts business across the five boroughs of New York (the

Bronx, Brooklyn, Queens, Manhattan, Staten Island). Each borough is honored with a cocktail. This recipe combines both sweet and dry vermouth with gin and orange peel. Over the years, more and more orange juice has been added to the recipe even though early recipes featured little or none. Some of the early recipes are vermouth heavy featuring equal parts gin, sweet and dry vermouths.

RONX

1 ounce gin
½ ounce dry vermouth
½ ounce sweet vermouth
½ ounce orange juice
1 dash of orange bitters
Orange twist

Add ice and water to a cocktail glass to chill the glass. Add ice to the tin side of a Boston shaker. In the mixing glass, add the dash of orange bitters, orange juice, sweet and dry vermouths, and the gin. Pour the contents of the mixing glass into the iced tin and secure the glass to the tin. Shake the contents until the ice sounds different and the contents are cold. Open the Boston shaker. Empty the cocktail glass, then strain the contents of the shaker into the empty glass. Take the orange peel and twist over the glass and gently rub the rim of the glass with the twist. Add the twist to the glass and serve.

Queens is the second most populated borough in New York City named for the Portuguese-born Queen of England, Scotland, and Ireland, Catherine, consort of King Charles II. This cocktail is like the Bronx cocktail but has pineapple instead of orange juice.

UEENS

1 ounce gin
½ ounce sweet vermouth
½ ounce dry vermouth
¾ ounce pineapple juice

Add ice and water to a cocktail glass to chill the glass. Add ice to the tin side of a Boston shaker. In the mixing glass, add pineapple juice, sweet and dry vermouths, and gin. Pour the contents of the mixing glass into the iced tin and secure the glass to the tin. Shake the contents until the ice sounds different and the contents are cold. Open the Boston shaker. Empty the cocktail glass, then strain the contents of the shaker into the empty glass. Serve.

Detroit has a lot to brag about including the creation of the Last Word cocktail at the Detroit Athletic Club before Prohibition. Detroit was a major hub for bootlegging action, and the club's bar remained open during Prohibition, so this cocktail was available to mobsters. A phrase you will never hear from a mobster: "Any last words?"

THE LAST WORD

1 ounce lime juice
1 ounce cherry-flavored liqueur
1 ounce Chartreuse
1 ounce gin
Cocktail cherry

Add ice and water to a cocktail glass to chill the glass. Add ice to a cocktail shaker. Add lime juice, cherry-flavored liqueur, Chartreuse, and gin to the cocktail shaker. Shake until you hear the ice change sound and the drink is cold. Empty the glass and strain the cocktail into the glass. Garnish with cocktail cherry.

US Senator Huey "The Kingfish" Long Jr. is perhaps the first politician in the country to endorse an alcoholic drink. Senator Long, a former governor of Louisiana, planned to run for president in 1936 but was assassinated in 1935. His favorite cocktail was invented by Henry Ramos at his bar. The drink was later adopted by the Roosevelt Hotel in New Orleans. This drink takes a long time to prepare but is well worth the effort.

AMOS GIN FIZZ

3 or 4 drops of orange flower water
1 egg white or 1 ounce egg whites
½ ounce simple syrup
½ ounce lemon juice
½ ounce lime juice
2 ounces heavy cream
1 ½ ounces gin

*Prepare a highball glass with ice to chill the glass. Add ice
to the shaker, then add orange flower water, egg white,
simple syrup, lemon and lime juice, heavy cream, and gin.
Shake for several minutes to ensure that the drink is fully
mixed. Refresh the highball glass with new ice and strain
the cocktail into the glass. Top with club soda and serve.*

When children are young, they are cute and full of potential;
they are little angels. However, when they grow up, some take
a wrong turn and end up in jail. A traditional Fallen Angel has
crème de menthe, but I substituted green Chartreuse. This is
a cocktail for the fallen.

ALLEN ANGEL

2 ounces gin
1 ounce lime juice
½ ounce green Chartreuse
1 dash Angostura bitters

Add ice and water to a cocktail glass to chill the glass. Add ice to the tin side of a Boston shaker. In the mixing glass, add Angostura bitters, green Chartreuse, lime juice, and gin. Pour the contents of the mixing glass into the iced tin and secure the glass to the tin. Shake the contents until the ice sounds different and the contents are cold. Open the Boston shaker. Empty the cocktail glass, then strain the contents of the shaker into the empty glass. Serve.

Lorraine Bracco shines when she works on acting projects where the subject is the mob. She was nominated for Best Supporting Actress Oscar for her role in *Goodfellas* and nominated for an Emmy several times for her role on *The Sopranos*. This cocktail was created by the bartending great Joe Gilmore after World War II for Charles de Gaulle's visit to Britain.

ORRAINE

1 ½ ounces gin
¾ ounce Lillet
¾ ounce Grand Marnier

Add ice and water to a cocktail glass to chill the glass. Add ice to the tin side of a Boston shaker. In the mixing glass, add gin, Lillet, and Grand Marnier. Pour the contents of the mixing glass into the iced tin and secure the glass to the tin. Shake the contents until the ice sounds different and the contents are cold. Open the Boston shaker. Empty the cocktail glass, then add a few ice cubes back into the glass, then strain the contents of the shaker into the empty glass. Serve.

The 1995 movie *Casino* reunites Robert De Niro and Joe Pesci with director Martin Scorsese from the 1990 hit *Goodfellas*. *Casino* features just how violent the mob can be (if you have a weak stomach, you might want to skip the end of the movie); the film is based on the real-life hit on Anthony and Michael Spilotro. The Casino cocktail is a wonderful mixture of Old Tom gin, maraschino liqueur, orange bitters, and lemon juice.

ASINO

1 ½ ounces Old Tom gin
¼ ounce maraschino liqueur
¼ ounce orange bitters
¼ ounce lemon juice
Lemon twist
Cocktail cherry

Add ice and water to a cocktail glass to chill the glass. Add ice to the tin side of a Boston shaker. In the mixing glass, add Old Tom gin, maraschino liqueur, orange bitters, and lemon juice. Pour the contents of the mixing glass into the iced tin and secure the glass to the tin. Shake the contents until the ice sounds different and the contents are cold. Open the Boston shaker. Empty the cocktail glass, then strain the contents of the shaker into the empty glass. Garnish with lemon twist and cocktail cherry. Serve.

The Clover Club cocktail was named for a traditional gentlemen's club in Philadelphia by the same name at the Bellevue-Stratford Hotel (which is now Hyatt at the Bellevue). The Clover Club cocktail was the signature cocktail of the establishment.

LOVER CLUB COCKTAIL

1 ½ ounces gin
½ ounce lemon juice
½ ounce raspberry syrup
½ ounce egg white

Add ice and water to a cocktail glass to chill the glass. In the mixing glass, add gin, lemon juice, raspberry syrup, and egg white. Pour the contents of the mixing glass into the tin and secure the glass to the tin. Shake the contents for one minute. Then add ice and shake again until the ice sounds different and the contents are cold. Open the Boston shaker. Empty the cocktail glass, then strain the contents of the shaker into the empty glass. Serve.

With a beautiful face, someone can get away with . . . well . . . murder. This cocktail is a tasty combination of three spirits.

NGEL FACE

1 ounce gin
1 ounce apricot brandy
1 ounce calvados

Add ice and water to a cocktail glass to chill the glass. Add ice to the tin side of a Boston shaker. In the mixing glass, add gin, apricot brandy, and calvados. Pour the contents of the mixing glass into the iced tin and secure the glass to the tin. Shake the contents until the ice sounds different and the contents are cold. Open the Boston shaker. Empty the cocktail glass, then strain the contents of the shaker into the empty glass. Serve.

The Gibson is a wonderful drink and a sibling of the martini. The only difference is the onion garnish. This drink is named for the independent and beautiful Gibson Girls of the early twentieth century. The name comes from the artist Charles Dana Gibson, who captured and defined ideal physical feminine attractiveness before World War I, about the same time the flapper look came in vogue. The benefit of ordering a Gibson instead of a martini is that cocktail onions are usually refrigerated, not left at room temperature like olives.

IBSON

¼ ounce extra dry vermouth
2 ½ ounces dry London gin
2 cocktail onions

Add ice and water to a cocktail glass to chill the glass. Add ice to the tin side of a Boston shaker. In the mixing glass, add vermouth and gin. Pour the contents of the mixing glass into the iced tin and secure the glass to the tin. Shake the contents until the ice sounds different and

the contents are cold. Open the Boston shaker. Empty the
cocktail glass, then strain the contents of the shaker into
the empty glass. Garnish with two cocktail onions. Serve.

RUM

Rum is made all over the world from sugar, sugar cane juice, molasses, or other sugar by-product. Rum is another bartender favorite because of the spirit's flexibility in cocktails. Rum comes in a wide spectrum of clear to brown colors based on how long the rum ages in oak barrels that have been charred on the inside. Most rum is distilled to a high proof and watered down to a market 80 proof (40 percent alcohol by volume). Some rum is sold at a higher "overproof" 151 proof (75.5 percent alcohol by volume). Rum was transported from the Caribbean islands to the United States during Prohibition or was made on homemade still in the United States.

RUM COCKTAILS

During Prohibition, one of the most complicated jobs was rum-running. The transportation of any liquor was illegal. So moving spirits on boats from the Caribbean, often from the island of Bimini, into US waters was dangerous regardless of whether the runner was caught. This drink celebrates those who risked the dangers of the open ocean and the bullets of the feds.

UMRUNNER

1 ½ ounces spiced rum
1 ounce orange juice
1 ounce pineapple juice
½ ounce lime juice
1 ounce crème de banana
½ ounce grenadine
1 orange slice or wedge
Ice

Add ice and water to a highball glass to chill the glass. Add ice to the tin side of a Boston shaker. In the mixing glass, add rum, orange juice, pineapple juice, lime juice, crème de banane, and grenadine. Pour the contents of the mixing glass into the iced tin and secure the glass to the tin. Shake the contents until the ice sounds different and the contents are cold. Open the Boston shaker. Empty the highball glass. Refill with ice, then strain the contents of the shaker into the glass. Garnish with orange slice or wedge. Serve.

"Cuba Libre" was a common cry during the Spanish-American War at the end of the nineteenth century. The United States assisted in freeing Cuba from Spanish control and took possession of Guam, Puerto Rico, and the Philippines. In the 1950s, Fidel Castro and Che Guevara overthrew the dictator Fulgencio Batista; this event is featured in the Academy Award–winning film *The Godfather, Part II*, during which

Michael Corleone decides not to invest family money in Cuba. This cocktail is simple to make and easy to drink.

UBA LIBRE

1 ½ ounces rum
4 ounces Coke
½ ounce fresh lime juice
Lime wedge

Add ice to an old-fashioned glass. To the glass, add lime juice, rum, and finally Coke. Garnish with lime wedge. Serve.

The combination of guns and bullets led to one thing: gunfire. The British Army combined hot tea or coffee with rum in the morning to begin the day. This drink also seems appropriate for the mob. If you try this one in the morning, be careful!

UNFIRE

8 ounces hot strong tea or hot coffee
1 ½ ounces rum

Prepare tea or coffee. Pour rum into a mug, then add the prepared tea or coffee and stir. Serve.

The pirate flag with the skull and crossbones is known as the Jolly Roger, but there are many versions of pirates' flags. The Buccaneers who sailed on ships under the Jolly Roger were engaged in an early form of organized crime. This drink is very appropriate, as it supplies a large portion of vitamin C, thanks to the lemon juice, which is very important to fight scurvy on long ship voyages.

JOLLY ROGER

2 ounces lemon juice
1 ounce rum
1 ounce crème de banane

Add ice and water to a wineglass to chill the glass. Add ice to the tin side of a Boston shaker. In the mixing glass, add lemon juice, rum, and crème de banane. Pour the contents of the mixing glass into the iced tin and secure the glass to the tin. Shake the contents until the ice sounds different and the contents are cold. Open the Boston shaker. Empty the wineglass, then fill the wineglass with ice. Strain the contents of the shaker into the ice-filled glass. Serve.

The Mafia has its own martini. This combination of rum with Chambord and apple juice is a tasty combination that will bring out your inner mobster.

AFIA MARTINI

2 ounces rum
½ ounce Chambord liqueur
1 ounce apple juice

Add ice and water to a cocktail glass to chill the glass. Add ice to the tin side of a Boston shaker. In the mixing glass, add rum, Chambord, and apple juice. Pour the contents of the mixing glass into the iced tin and secure the glass to the tin. Shake the contents until the ice sounds different and the contents are cold. Open the Boston shaker. Empty the cocktail glass, then strain the contents of the shaker into the empty glass. Serve.

Whenever you cut a deal, you should ask for the money first!

IRST THE MONEY

1 ounce dark rum
½ ounce coffee liqueur
1 barspoon white crème de menthe
1 ounce fresh squeezed lime juice
4 ounces Coke
Lime wedge

Add ice and water to a highball glass to chill the glass. Add ice to the tin side of a Boston shaker. In the mixing glass, add rum, coffee liqueur, crème de menthe, and lime juice. Pour the contents of the mixing glass into the iced tin and secure the glass to the tin. Shake the contents until the ice sounds different and the contents are cold. Open the Boston shaker. Empty the highball glass, add ice, and then strain the contents of the shaker into the empty glass. Top with Coke and garnish with lime. Serve.

Life in the mob is not easy; in fact, it is full of pain. Every so often, you might need a painkiller. This one is easy to drink and is sure to work. The Pusser's Rum company holds the trademark to the Pain Killer®.

AIN KILLER®

2 ounces Pusser's Rum
4 ounces pineapple juice
1 ounce cream of coconut

1 ounce orange juice
Freshly grated nutmeg

Add ice and water to a highball glass to chill the glass. Add ice to the tin side of a Boston shaker. In the mixing glass, add Pusser's Rum, pineapple juice, cream of coconut, and orange juice. Pour the contents of the mixing glass into the iced tin and secure the glass to the tin. Shake the contents until the ice sounds different and the contents are cold. Open the Boston shaker. Empty the highball glass, then add ice and strain the contents of the shaker into the ice-filled glass. Grate fresh nutmeg over the top. Serve.

A true Dark 'n Stormy® includes both Gosling's Black Seal Rum and Gosling's Stormy Ginger Beer. Gosling's is located on the island of Bermuda. Depending on how Dark 'n Stormy® you want your drink to be, Gosling's sells an 80 proof, 140 proof, and 151 proof.

ARK 'N STORMY®

1 ½ ounces Gosling's Black Seal Rum
5 ounces Gosling's Stormy Ginger Beer
Lime slice

*Add ice to a highball glass. Add rum, then the
ginger beer. Stir gently. Add lime wedge to
the side of the glass for garnish. Serve.*

The mob interacted with the Cuban government to secure hotels and casinos. The decider on these transactions was El Presidente, who could always use a cut of mob profits so that the deal would go through.

L PRESIDENTE

1 ½ ounces rum
1 ounce dry vermouth
⅓ ounce orange liqueur
¼ ounce grenadine
Cocktail cherry

Add ice and water to a cocktail glass to chill the glass. Add ice to the tin side of a Boston shaker. In the mixing glass, add rum, vermouth, orange liqueur, and grenadine. Pour the contents of the mixing glass into the iced tin and secure the glass to the tin. Shake the contents until the ice sounds different and the contents are cold. Open the Boston shaker. Empty the cocktail glass, then strain the contents of the shaker into the empty glass. Add cocktail cherry for garnish. Serve.

Staten Island is one of the five boroughs of New York City and the least populated. This is a nice cocktail that is great to sip on a hot summer day with thoughts of a tropical island—even though Staten Island is not.

 STATEN ISLAND FERRY

2 ounces coconut rum
6 ounces pineapple juice

Add ice to a highball glass to chill the glass. Add ice to the tin side of a Boston shaker. In the mixing glass, add coconut rum and pineapple juice. Pour the contents of the mixing glass into the iced tin and secure the glass to the tin. Shake the contents until the ice sounds different and the contents are cold. Open the Boston shaker. Strain the contents of the shaker into the iced glass. Serve.

TEQUILA AND MESCAL

Tequila and mescal are both made from the agave plant. The agave plant takes between eight to twelve years to reach maturity, which means tequila makers must project a decade in advance the demand for tequila. Like rum, tequila is aged to varying degrees in burned oak barrels. Blanco or plata is tequila that is aged less than two months in stainless steel or neutral oak barrels. Joven or oro is generally unaged tequila that is flavored with caramel coloring. Reposado is tequila that is aged a minimum of two months but less than a year in oak barrels. Añejo is tequila that is aged for a minimum of one year but less than three years in oak barrels. Finally, Extra Añejo is aged for a minimum of three years in oak barrels. The longer that tequila is aged, the darker the liquid becomes and the more influence the wood has on the flavor. Also, the longer that tequila is aged, the higher the price of the tequila. Just as rum was moved from the Caribbean into the United States, so was tequila moved across the southern border of the United States.

TEQUILA AND MESCAL COCKTAILS

The mob uses bombs when they want to get rid of someone remotely. This cocktail will do the same if you are not careful.

BROOKLYN BOMBER

1 ounce tequila
½ ounce Cointreau
½ ounce cherry brandy
½ ounce Galliano

1 ounce lemon juice
Orange slice
Cocktail cherry

Add ice to a hurricane glass to chill the glass. Add ice to the tin side of a Boston shaker. In the mixing glass, add lemon juice, Galliano, cherry brandy, Cointreau, and tequila. Pour the contents of the mixing glass into the iced tin and secure the glass to the tin. Shake the contents until the ice sounds different and the contents are cold. Open the Boston shaker. Strain the contents of the shaker into the ice-filled hurricane glass. Garnish with orange slice and cherry. Serve.

The devil made me do it! This cocktail, which is a distant cousin to the margarita, is easy to drink. The devil is in how easy this drink goes down.

E DIABLO COCKTAIL

1 ½ ounces tequila
½ ounce crème de cassis
½ ounce lime juice
3 ounces ginger beer
Lime wedge

Add ice to a highball glass to chill the glass. Add ice to the tin side of a Boston shaker. In the mixing glass, add tequila, crème de cassis, and lime juice. Pour the contents of the mixing glass into the iced tin and secure the glass to the tin. Shake the contents until the ice sounds different and the contents are cold. Open the Boston shaker. Strain the contents of the shaker into the ice-filled glass. Top with ginger beer. Stir gently. Garnish with lime wedge. Serve.

Tom Collins has many cousins. Juan is one of them. The Collins family of drinks is sour long drinks which are perfect for any occasion. Replace the tequila with Old Tom Gin to meet Tom Collins or gin to meet John Collins.

JUAN COLLINS

1 ½ ounces tequila
1 ounce lemon juice
½ ounce agave syrup with ½ ounce water added
Club soda
Lime wedge
Cocktail cherry

Add ice to a collins glass to chill the glass. Add tequila,
lemon juice, and watered-down agave syrup. Top with club
soda and garnish with lime and cocktail cherry. Serve.

Mobsters might meet at a bullfight to discuss business like in the 2005 movie *The Matador*, which stars Pierce Brosnan and Gregg Kinnear, about an assassin who strikes up a friendship with a businessman.

MATADOR

1 ½ ounces tequila
3 ounces pineapple juice
½ ounce lime juice

Add ice and water to a cocktail glass to chill the glass. Add ice to the tin side of a Boston shaker. In the mixing glass, add tequila, pineapple juice, and lime juice. Pour the contents of the mixing glass into the iced tin and secure the glass to the tin. Shake the contents until the ice sounds different and the contents are cold. Open the Boston shaker. Empty the cocktail glass, then strain the contents of the shaker into the empty glass. Serve.

When it comes to women, for mobsters it is hands off; in fact, even looking without "going on the record" can mean serious consequences. There are none as beautiful as the perfect margarita.

ARGARITA

1 ½ ounces tequila	Lime wedge
¾ ounce Cointreau	Lime slice
¾ ounce lime juice	Kosher salt for the rim

Add ice and water to a margarita glass to chill the glass. Set up a plate of kosher salt. Add ice to the tin side of a Boston shaker. In the mixing glass, add tequila, Cointreau, and lime juice. Pour the contents of the mixing glass into the iced tin and secure the glass to the tin. Shake the contents until the ice sounds different and the contents are cold. Open the Boston shaker. Empty the cocktail glass. Take the lime wedge and wipe the outside of the glass. Gently place the side of the glass into the salt, then strain the contents of the shaker into the empty glass. Garnish with lime. Serve.

Another Mexican beauty is paloma. Easy to make and easy to drink.

ALOMA

2 ounces tequila
8 ounces grapefruit soda
Lime wedge

Add ice to a highball glass to chill the glass. Add tequila and then grapefruit soda. Garnish with lime wedge. Serve.

Omertà is a powerful oath. Some mobsters take information to their grave but many go in to the program. These rats are also called snitches. The snitch is also a riff on the Paloma.

HE SNITCH

1 ½ ounces mescal
¼ ounce Campari
1 ounce grapefruit shrub
½ ounce lime juice
½ ounce simple syrup
Pinch of salt
Grapefruit twist

Add ice to an old-fashioned glass to chill the glass. Add ice to the tin side of a Boston shaker. In the mixing glass, add mescal, Campari, grapefruit shrub, lime juice, simple syrup, and pinch of salt. Pour the contents of the

mixing glass into the iced tin and secure the glass to the tin. Shake the contents until the ice sounds different and the contents are cold. Open the Boston shaker. Strain the contents of the shaker into the ice-filled old-fashioned glass. Garnish with grapefruit twist. Serve.

Every sunrise and sunset is beautiful. A sunrise means that you get to live another day. With this sunrise, you get to enjoy tequila, too.

EQUILA SUNRISE

1 ½ ounces tequila
3 ounces orange juice
½ ounce grenadine syrup
Orange slice
Cocktail cherry

Add ice to an old-fashioned glass to chill the glass. Add tequila and orange juice. Add grenadine syrup, which will sink to the bottom of the glass, then stir gently. Serve.

You should be passionate about something or someone. Passion makes life interesting. There is a bite and grit to passion. Mobsters are passionate. The passion cocktail is a cosmopolitan made with tequila instead of vodka, so expect this cocktail to have a little more bite and grit.

PASSION COCKTAIL VERSUS THE COSMOPOLITAN

1 ounce tequila
1 ½ ounces cranberry juice
½ ounce lime juice
1 ounce Cointreau
Lime slice

Add ice and water to a cocktail glass to chill the glass. Add ice to the tin side of a Boston shaker. In the mixing glass, add tequila, cranberry juice, lime juice, and Cointreau. Pour the contents of the mixing glass into the iced tin and secure the glass to the tin. Shake the contents until the ice sounds different and the contents are cold. Open the Boston shaker. Empty the cocktail glass, then strain the contents of the shaker into the empty glass. Garnish with lime wedge. Serve.

You may hear a mobster pray a Hail Mary or an Ave Maria after committing a sin or before his death. A well-made vodka bloody mary is amazing, but a bloody maria is divine.

▛LOODY MARIA VERSUS BLOODY MARY

2 ounces tequila
5 ounces tomato juice
½ ounce lime juice
4 dashes Worcestershire sauce
3 dashes Tabasco sauce
½ tablespoon horseradish
Celery salt
Finely ground pepper
Jicama spear
Jalapeño

Add ice to a highball glass to chill the glass. Add ice to the tin side of a Boston shaker. In the mixing glass, add tequila, tomato juice, lime juice, Worcestershire sauce, Tabasco sauce, horseradish, celery salt, and ground pepper. Pour the contents of the mixing glass into the iced tin. Then roll them back into the mixing glass. Repeat this process at least three times. Strain the bloody maria into the highball glass with ice. Garnish with jicama spear and jalapeño. Serve.

A mule is someone who carries illicit product from one location to another. A mule can also refer to a tasty drink made with ginger beer and lime. If you are a fan of the Moscow mule, you might want to try a Mayan mule. Just substitute the vodka with tequila or mescal.

AYAN MULE VERSUS MOSCOW MULE

1 ounce lime juice (reserve one-half of the lime for garnish)
½ ounce simple syrup
1 ½ ounces tequila or mescal
4 ounces ginger beer

Add ice to an old-fashioned glass or a copper mug to chill the glass. Add lime juice, simple syrup, and tequila. Stir to mix the three ingredients. Add ginger beer and stir gently. Garnish with lime peel. Serve.

BRANDY

Wine is distilled into brandy. Most brandy is aged for at least a little time, even if there is no color influence from the oak barrel in which the brandy is aged. Cognac, Armagnac, and calvados are three examples of famous French brandy. Both cognac and Armagnac start as grape wine, whereas calvados begins as apple wine. The longer the brandy is aged, the higher its price. Brandy is also made in North and South America. Brandy was well known to the Mafia for many reasons. It is something that the Mafia would have a great interest in moving into the United States.

BRANDY COCKTAILS

The Second City is second to none in many respects. At one time, Chicago was the home base for Al Capone and his American boys who may have pulled off one of the most infamous unsolved crimes, the Saint Valentine's Day Massacre. This cocktail dates to the time when Al Capone ruled the Windy City's underworld.

THE CHICAGO COCKTAIL

2 ounces brandy
1 dash aromatic bitters
¼ ounce Cointreau
1 ounce sparkling wine (optional)

Add ice into an old-fashioned glass.
Add dash of bitters, Cointreau, and brandy.
Top with sparkling wine if desired. Serve.

If only we could turn back time, but then again, some mobsters might not like some of the people whom they have whacked coming back to life. This drink just might do it.

THE CORPSE REVIVER

1 ½ ounces brandy
1 ounce sweet vermouth
1 ounce calvados
Orange twist

Add ice and water to a cocktail glass to chill the glass. Add ice to the tin side of a Boston shaker. In the mixing glass, add brandy, vermouth, and calvados. Pour the contents of the mixing glass into the iced tin and secure the glass to the tin. Shake the contents until the ice sounds different and the contents are cold. Open the Boston shaker. Empty the cocktail glass, then strain the contents of the shaker into the empty glass. Garnish with orange twist. Serve.

Climbing the ladder to success, there are several bench marks: first car, college degree, first house. However, one of the last bench marks is having a Fifth Avenue address. Of course, you can take the shortcut and steal or just inherit the address. There is no shortcut on the Fifth Avenue cocktail, though. Practice makes perfect.

IFTH AVENUE

1 ounce brown crème de cacao
1 ounce apricot brandy
1 ounce light cream

Make sure that the glass you use has straight sides. Pour in the crème de cacao. Use the back of a barspoon and pour the apricot brandy over slowly so that the brandy floats on top of the crème de cacao. Repeat with the cream. When the three layers are achieved, serve.

To the mattress and/or between the sheets. Mobsters go to the mattress to lie low when warring with a rival family, but they spend time between the sheets with their *comare*.

BETWEEN THE SHEETS

1 ½ ounces brandy
1 ounce rum
½ ounce Cointreau
½ ounce simple syrup
½ ounce fresh squeezed lemon juice

Add ice and water to a cocktail glass to chill the glass. Add ice to the tin side of a Boston shaker. In the mixing glass, add brandy, rum, Cointreau, lemon juice, and simple syrup. Pour the contents of the mixing glass into the iced tin and secure the glass to the tin. Shake the contents until the ice sounds different and the contents are cold. Open the Boston shaker. Empty the cocktail glass, then strain the contents of the shaker into the empty glass. Serve.

Don't ever offend a mobster or you might be hanging from the rafters.

FROM THE RAFTERS

1 ounce brandy
1 ounce Cointreau
1 ounce pineapple juice

¼ ounce Frangelico
Cocktail cherry

Add ice and water to a cocktail glass to chill the glass. Add ice to the tin side of a Boston shaker. In the mixing glass, add brandy, Cointreau, pineapple juice, and Frangelico. Pour the contents of the mixing glass into the iced tin and secure the glass to the tin. Shake the contents until the ice sounds different and the contents are cold. Open the Boston shaker. Empty the cocktail glass, then strain the contents of the shaker into the empty glass. Garnish with cocktail cherry. Serve.

A painful blow from a mobster can be a stinger, something to fear. A cocktail stinger is delightful. Just watch out!

TINGER

1 ½ ounces brandy
½ ounce white crème de menthe
Fresh mint

Add ice and water to a cocktail glass to chill the glass. Add ice to the tin side of a Boston shaker. In the mixing glass, add brandy and crème de menthe. Pour the contents of the mixing glass into the iced tin and secure the glass to the tin. Shake the contents until the ice sounds different and the contents are cold. Open the Boston shaker. Empty the cocktail glass, then strain the contents of the shaker into the empty glass. Lightly slap the fresh mint on the back of your hand. Garnish the drink with the mint. Serve.

Similar to the Manhattan, the metropolitan uses spirits and vermouth to make a wonderful drink. Most mobsters do business in a metropolitan area or a city and the surrounding area.

 ETROPOLITAN

2 ounces brandy
1 ounce sweet vermouth
2 dashes Angostura bitters
Cocktail cherry

Add ice and water to a cocktail glass to chill the glass. Add ice to the tin side of a Boston shaker. In the mixing glass, add Angostura bitters, brandy, and vermouth. Pour the contents of the mixing glass into the iced tin and secure the glass to the tin. Shake the contents until the ice sounds different and the contents are cold. Open the Boston shaker. Empty the cocktail glass, then strain the contents of the shaker into the empty glass. Garnish with cocktail cherry. Serve.

A horse named Khartoum. "You do appreciate beauty, don't you? Six hundred thousand dollars on four hoofs—I bet Russian czars never paid that kind of dough for a single horse." In the 1972 film *The Godfather*, Jack Woltz bragged to Tom Hagen about his horse. Hagen asked for a favor for Don Corleone, but after refusing, Woltz ends up waking up in bed with his prize horse's head. One of the Oscars that the film won was for Best Adapted Screenplay for Francis Ford Coppola and Mario Puzo, who also authored the novel. The horse's name references Major-General Charles George Gordon, a.k.a. Gordon of Khartoum, who was beheaded during the Siege of Khartoum in 1885.

HE HORSE'S NECK

1 ½ ounces brandy
4 ounces ginger ale
1 dash Angostura bitters
Lemon twist

Add ice to a highball glass. Add Angostura bitters, brandy, and ginger ale. Stir gently and garnish with a long lemon twist. Serve.

Similar to the sidecar, this is one of the six cocktails that everyone should know how to make according to David Embury.

ACK ROSE

2 ounces apple brandy
½ ounce fresh squeezed lemon juice
¼ ounce grenadine
Superfine sugar

Set up the cocktail glasses ahead of time. Dip the edge of the cocktail glass in water, then dip in a plate of superfine sugar for a thin even frost on the edge of the glass. Then freeze the glassware. Add ice to the tin side of a Boston shaker. In the mixing glass, add apple brandy, lemon

juice, and grenadine. Pour the contents of the mixing glass into the iced tin and secure the glass to the tin. Shake the contents until the ice sounds different and the contents are cold. Open the Boston shaker. Strain the contents of the shaker into the empty glass. Serve.

Panama has long been seen as a tax haven. This is where many mobsters conduct their banking—as was made clear by the Panama Papers. In addition to mobsters' transactions, the financial dealings of many other people, from many countries were also exposed.

PANAMA

1 ounce brandy
1 ounce white crème de cacao
1 ounce cream

Add ice and water to a cocktail glass to chill the glass. Add ice to the tin side of a Boston shaker. In the mixing glass, add brandy, white crème de cacao, and cream. Pour the contents of the mixing glass into the iced tin and secure the glass to the tin. Shake the contents until the ice sounds different and the contents are cold. Open the Boston shaker. Empty the cocktail glass, then strain the contents of the shaker into the empty glass. Serve.

WHISKEY

Whiskey is the largest differentiated spirit category. This spirit was made in Scotland, Ireland, Canada, and the United States long before Prohibition. Whiskey is distilled from beer made from grain. Each tradition uses different grain or a grain mixture for the distiller's beer. The beer is then distilled into a clear spirit and aged in oak barrels for a short or extended period. The longer the whiskey is aged, the higher the price of the spirit. Most Scotch whiskey is made from malt and grain whiskeys and is aged in a variety of used barrels including bourbon, sherry, and porto barrels. Scotch has a unique smoked peaty flavor and aroma. Most Scotch is aged for at least four years but can be aged for much longer. Irish whiskey has a light and mild flavor and aroma and can be made from a variety of grains. This spirit is aged for at least three years but much is aged longer. Canadian whiskey is mild flavored, made from multiple grains, and is aged for at least three years. Bourbon is one of the most highly regulated whiskeys that is made in the United States (95 percent is made in Kentucky). It is made from 51 percent corn (most bourbon distillers use more, closer to 65–75 percent). As bourbon comes off the still, it must be less than 160 proof, and only water can be added to bourbon. As bourbon is added to newly charred oak barrels, it cannot be more than 125 proof or less than 80 proof. There is no minimum age for bourbon, but if the bourbon is aged less than two years, there must be an age statement on the label. Most bourbon is aged for at least four years. Some of the bourbon distillers remained open during Prohibition to make medicinal bourbon (yes, you could visit a doctor and receive a prescription for bourbon during Prohibition). Tennessee whiskey is made in Tennessee with all the regulations of bourbon and the addition of the Lincoln County process, which involves a maple charcoal filter. As Prohibition arrived in Tennessee early (1911), Jack Daniels moved to Saint Louis, and George Dickel moved north to Kentucky. Other whiskeys are usually defined by the grain from which they are primarily made. For example, corn whiskey is at least 80 percent corn, rye whiskey is at least 51 percent rye, and wheat whiskey is at least 51 percent wheat.

WHISKEY COCKTAILS

The word *Manhattan*, which refers to the island and borough of New York City, may originate from the Leni-Lenape word that means "the place where we got drunk." If this is the case, the name for the Manhattan cocktail is ironic. The Rob Roy cocktail is named for the Scottish folk hero and outlaw Rob Roy MacGregor. Part of MacGregor legacy includes a bloody battle that he waged against James Graham, 1st Duke of Montrose. MacGregor defaulted on a debt related to a loan Montrose had extended MacGregor for cattle. MacGregor was eventually pardoned. Liam Neeson played the title character in the 1995 movie *Rob Roy*. John Hurt played a wonderful Montrose, and Tim Roth received an Academy Award nomination for his role as the evil and conniving Archibald Cunningham.

THE MANHATTAN VERSUS THE ROB ROY

2 ounces rye whiskey (or bourbon)
 (Scotch whiskey for Rob Roy)
1 ounce sweet vermouth
1 dash Angostura bitters
1 dash Peychaud's bitters
Cocktail cherry

Add ice and water to a cocktail glass to chill the glass. Add ice to a mixing glass, then add both bitters, whiskey, and vermouth. Stir at least forty times. Empty the cocktail glass, then strain the contents of the mixing glass into the empty cocktail glass. Garnish with cherry. Serve.

Brooklyn has the highest population of any of the boroughs in New York City. This cocktail is similar to the dry Manhattan but includes orange bitters and maraschino liqueur.

THE BROOKLYN

2 ounces rye whiskey
1 ounce dry vermouth
¼ ounce maraschino liqueur
3 dashes orange bitters
Lemon twist

Add ice and water to a cocktail glass to chill the glass. Add ice to the tin side of a Boston shaker. In the mixing glass, add rye whiskey, vermouth, maraschino liqueur, and orange bitters. Pour the contents of the mixing glass into the iced tin and secure the glass to the tin. Shake the contents until the ice sounds different and the contents are cold. Open the Boston shaker. Empty the cocktail glass, then strain the contents of the shaker into the empty glass. Garnish with lemon twist. Serve.

The original cocktail was created in Elmsford, New York, at the beginning of the Revolutionary War. We view them as heroes now, but the founding fathers of the United States were criminals when they signed the Declaration of Independence.

THE OLD FASHIONED

¼ ounce simple syrup
2–3 dashes of Angostura bitters
2 ounces bourbon
Orange slice
Cocktail cherry

Pour the simple syrup into the bottom of an old-fashioned glass followed by the bitters. Add ice to the glass and stir. Garnish with orange slice and cocktail cherry. Serve.

A president of the United States can be a criminal, even though he made the famous denial, "I am not a crook." His successor, President Gerald Ford, would pardon the former president. This cocktail was created during happier times, at the beginning of his presidency on a state visit to Great Britain by the head barman at the Savoy hotel's American Bar.

NIXON

1 ½ ounces bourbon
1 ½ ounces sloe gin
3 dashes peach bitters

Slice of fresh peach
Cocktail cherry

Add ice to an old-fashioned glass to chill the glass. Add ice to the tin side of a Boston shaker. In the mixing glass, add peach bitters, sloe gin, and bourbon. Pour the contents of the mixing glass into the iced tin, and roll the contents back and forth at least three times. Strain the contents of the shaker into the ice-filled glass. Serve.

The boulevardier is a fun drink. Similar to the negroni, the boulevardier features bourbon as the spirit instead of gin for the negroni. To be clear, they are different drinks but at the same time similar. Another similar drink is the Old Pal, which features rye whiskey as the spirit and dry vermouth served up in a cocktail glass with a lemon twist.

OULEVARDIER VERSUS THE NEGRONI

1 ounce bourbon
1 ounce sweet vermouth
1 ounce Campari
Orange peel

Add ice to an old-fashioned glass to chill the glass. Add ice to a mixing glass, then add bourbon, vermouth, and the Campari. Stir at least thirty or forty times. Strain the contents of the mixing glass into the ice-filled glass. Twist the orange peel above the drink and wipe it on the rim of the glass. You can discard or serve the orange peel with the drink. Serve.

The Vieux Carré cocktail was invented at the Carousel Piano Bar and Lounge at the Hotel Monteleone in New Orleans. The drink features the history of the Big Easy in a glass. *The Big Easy* is also the name of a 1987 film that features Dennis Quaid as police lieutenant Remy McSwain. In the opening scene, McSwain is called to investigate a murder at the Piazza d'Italia where he "makes" the "dead meat" as "wise guy, scum bag" Freddy Angelo, who works for Vinnie "The Cannon" DiMotti, the mob boss in New Orleans. The placement of the body in the fountain sent a message to DiMotti from the unknown killer.

IEUX CARRÉ

2 dashes Peychaud's bitters
2 dashes Angostura bitters
1 barspoon Bénédictine
1 ounce rye whiskey
1 ounce cognac
1 ounce sweet vermouth
Lemon twist

Add ice to an old-fashioned glass to chill the glass. Add ice to a mixing glass, then add both bitters, Bénédictine, rye, cognac, and vermouth. Stir at least thirty or forty times. Strain the contents of the mixing glass into the ice-filled glass. Twist the lemon twist above the drink and wipe it on the rim of the glass. Serve the lemon twist with the drink. Serve.

Ward Eight refers to a political voting area in Boston. Martin Lomasney controlled Ward Eight. He was known to say, "Never write if you can speak; never speak if you can nod; never nod if you can wink."

 ## ARD EIGHT

2 ounces rye whiskey
½ ounce lemon juice
½ ounce orange juice
1 teaspoon grenadine
Cocktail cherry

Add ice and water to a cocktail glass to chill the glass. Add ice to the tin side of a Boston shaker. In the mixing glass, add rye whiskey, lemon juice, orange juice, and grenadine. Pour the contents of the mixing glass into the iced tin and secure the glass to the tin. Shake the contents until the ice sounds different and the contents are cold. Open the Boston shaker. Empty the cocktail glass, then strain the contents of the shaker into the empty glass. Garnish with cocktail cherry. Serve.

The mint julep is the drink of the Kentucky Derby. The track—any track, for that matter—will attract mobsters. They like to blend in, so many have had mint juleps.

HE MINT JULEP

¼ ounce simple syrup
4–6 mint leaves

2–3 ounces bourbon
Mint sprig

Add simple syrup to a pewter or silver julep cup. Lay the leaves out on your palm and lightly smack them with your other hand. Add them to the cup. Add bourbon and mix. Then add crushed ice. Smack the mint sprig between your hands and add to the julep. Serve.

The Sazerac, "the official cocktail of New Orleans," competes with the old fashioned as the original cocktail. If true, the cocktail is a Spanish or French invention, not an American one, as Spain controlled New Orleans from 1763 until 1802 and France from 1718 until 1763 and 1802 until 1803. The original Sazerac featured cognac, but the phylloxera plague made it necessary to substitute rye.

AZERAC

⅓ ounce absinthe
¼ ounce simple syrup
2 dashes Peychaud's bitters
2 ounces rye whiskey (or cognac)
Lemon peel

Add ice and water to an old-fashioned glass to chill the glass. Once chilled, add absinthe to the glass and swirl to cover the sides of the glass. Discard the excess absinthe. Add simple syrup to the bottom of the glass followed by the bitters. Add rye whiskey to the glass, then ice. Stir. Twist the lemon twist above the drink and wipe it on the rim of the glass. Serve the lemon twist with the drink. Serve.

Sometimes you just need a shot. You might try "the three wise men" or "the four horsemen," depending on what kind of day you experience.

THE THREE WISE MEN VERSUS THE FOUR HORSEMEN

½ ounce Scotch whiskey
½ ounce Tennessee whiskey
½ ounce bourbon

Prepare a glass with ice. Add the three whiskeys to the glass. Stir and serve. For the four horsemen, add ½ ounce Irish whiskey.

Cool, refreshing, and intoxicating, the whiskey sour is the perfect cocktail for the hot days of summer.

 **HISKEY SOUR**

1 ½ ounces whiskey
1 ounce lemon juice
½ ounce simple syrup
¼ ounce egg white
Dash Angostura bitters
Orange slice
Cocktail cherry

Add ice and water to a cocktail glass to chill the glass. Add ice to the tin side of a Boston shaker. In the mixing glass, add Angostura bitters, whiskey, lemon juice, simple syrup, and egg white. Pour the contents of the mixing glass into the iced tin and secure the glass to the tin. Shake the contents until the ice sounds different and the contents are cold. Open the Boston shaker. Empty the cocktail glass, then strain the contents of the shaker into the empty glass. Garnish with orange slice and cocktail cherry. Serve.

Blood and sand sounds like a mob-inspired cocktail. However, the cocktail was inspired by a silent movie by the same name that featured everyone's favorite paramour Rudolph Valentino. Valentino's behavior would not have been tolerated by the mob unless he "goes on the record" to say that he did not initiate contact with the female. No sense in getting whacked for love; much safer to drink this cocktail.

BLOOD AND SAND

1 ounce orange juice
1 ounce sweet vermouth
1 ounce cherry-flavored liqueur
1 ounce blended Scotch whiskey
Cocktail cherry

Add ice and water to a cocktail glass. Add ice to a cocktail shaker. Then add orange juice, sweet vermouth, cherry-flavored liqueur, and blended Scotch whiskey. Close the shaker and shake until the ice sounds different and the drink is cold. Empty the ice from the cocktail glass, then strain the cocktail into the glass. Garnish with cherry. Serve.

BEER, WINE, AND LIQUEURS

Modern alcoholic concoctions can be made from beer, wine, and liqueurs. Beer and wine are naturally fermented beverages. Beer is made from grains, usually barley, and generally ferments to about 5 percent alcohol by volume, although beer can range from a low alcohol content to a high 11 percent alcohol by volume. Wine is made from fruit, usually grapes, and generally ferments to about 12.5 percent alcohol by volume, although wine can range from a low 5 percent to a high 15 percent alcohol by volume. Fortified wine is wine that has added spirit, usually brandy, and enjoys an even higher alcohol content. Liqueurs are flavored, sweetened alcoholic beverage that are featured in many cocktails and served as stand-alone after-dinner drinks also known as cordials. The alcohol by volume range for most liqueurs is from 17 percent (34 proof) to 30 percent (60 proof) but can be higher than 50 percent (100 proof).

OTHER COCKTAILS

Long Island iced tea is a perfect way to hide your alcohol in plain sight and give the impression that you are drinking nonalcoholic iced tea.

ONG ISLAND ICED TEA

½ ounce tequila
½ ounce vodka
½ ounce white rum
½ ounce gin
½ ounce triple sec
1 ounce lemon juice
1 ounce simple syrup
Splash of Coke

Add ice to a highball glass to chill the glass. Then build the drink in the glass. Add tequila, vodka, rum, gin, triple sec, lemon juice, and simple syrup. Stir the drink, then add a splash of Coke for color and stir again. Garnish with a slice of lemon and serve.

Do you look for snakes when you open the mailbox? People who are worried about being whacked might be careful. This cocktail is the best type of snakebite to get.

SNAKEBITE

8–10 ounces cider
8–10 ounces stout

In a pint glass, pour 8–10 ounces of cider, then float 8–10 ounces of stout on top. Serve.

America is a great country! Only in America could Italian Primo Carnera win the World Heavyweight Championship. A drink was created referencing the country where he won the title.

AMERICANO

1 ounce Campari
1 ounce sweet vermouth
Orange slice

Add ice to an old-fashioned glass to chill the glass. Pour in the Campari and sweet vermouth. Stir. Garnish with orange slice. Serve.

Mobsters always have to worry that their car is rigged to blow up. This version of the boilermaker features all Irish products.

RISH CAR BOMB

10 ounces stout
½ ounce Irish whiskey
½ ounce Irish cream liqueur

Set up the Irish whiskey and the Irish cream in the same shot glass by floating the whiskey on top of the Irish cream. Then pour 10 ounces of stout in a pint glass. Carefully drop the shot glass into the pint glass. Serve.

Many mobsters call for a hit in the afternoon.

EATH IN THE AFTERNOON

1 ounce absinthe
5 ounces champagne

Add absinthe into a sparkling wineglass and top with champagne. Serve.

There are two Prince of Wales cocktails. The first is named for Albert Edward, Prince of Wales, the future Edward VII, son of Queen Victoria and Prince Albert. The second is named for Charles Phillip Arthur George, Prince of Wales, son of Queen Elizabeth II and Prince Phillip. The second cocktail was created by bartender Joe Gilmore to mark the investiture of the current holder of that title. Charles surpassed his great-great-grandfather Edward VII as the longest serving Prince of Wales in history in 2017. Edward VII's grandson and Charles's great-uncle, Edward Albert Christian George Andrew Patrick David, Prince of Wales, was in a New York speakeasy during the 1920s when the police staged a raid. The prince was saved by the club hostess, Texas Guinan, who moved him into the kitchen, put a chef's toque on his head, and had him cook eggs until the raid was over. Later, the prince would rule as Edward VIII, but a relationship with an American divorcée, Wallis Simpson, made it necessary for him to abdicate in favor of his brother, George VI, who granted him the title Duke of Windsor.

# PRINCE OF WALES #1

1 ½ ounces rye
1 ounce champagne
1 small piece of pineapple
1 dash Angostura bitters

¼ teaspoon maraschino liqueur
1 teaspoon simple syrup

Add ice and water to a sparkling wineglass to chill the glass. Add ice to the tin side of a Boston shaker. In the mixing glass, add Angostura bitters, rye, pineapple, simple syrup, and maraschino liqueur. Pour the contents of the mixing glass into the iced tin and secure the glass to the

*tin. Shake the contents until the ice sounds different and
the contents are cold. Open the Boston shaker. Empty
the sparkling wineglass, then strain the contents of the
shaker into the empty glass. Top with champagne. Serve.*

RINCE OF WALES #2

1 ounce lemon juice
1 ounce cherry brandy
1 strawberry

1 teaspoon simple syrup
5 ounces champagne

*Blend the lemon juice, brandy, strawberry, and
simple syrup together. Pour into a sparkling
wineglass and top with champagne.*

The Seelbach Hotel was home to none other than Al "Scarface" Capone when he visited Louisville, Kentucky, on business. Lucky Luciano and Dutch Schultz also enjoyed the com-
forts of this hotel. F. Scott Fitzgerald used the splendor and
elegance of the place for inspiration for his novel *The Great
Gatsby.* Master mixologist Adam Segar used all the lore as
inspiration for the Seelbach cocktail, then in a mobster-style
twist he lied about the cocktail's origin. As the director of
restaurants at the historic hotel, claimed that in 1995 he
discovered the recipe for the cocktail that was created by a
pre-Prohibition bartender at the Seelbach. The story seemed
so viable that everyone believed the lie for more than twenty
years. In 2016, Segar finally admitted the truth to the *New
York Times* as he opened the Tuck Room in Manhattan.

THE SEELBACH COCKTAIL

7 dashes Angostura
    bitters
7 dashes Peychaud's
    bitters

1 ounce bourbon whiskey
½ ounce Cointreau
4–5 ounces champagne
Lemon twist

Add ice to a mixing glass. Then add bitters, bourbon, and Cointreau. Stir until cold. Strain into a sparkling wine flute and add champagne until full. Serve.

For those in mourning, try the Black Velvet. You don't want to be disrespectful and champagne is all about celebration. So pull a black veil over your sparkling wine with a little stout. First created to mourn Great Britain's Prince Albert, Queen Victoria's prince consort, this cocktail is also appropriate for a mobster funeral.

BLACK VELVET

4 ounces stout
4 ounces champagne

Pour champagne into a sparkling wine flute glass, then top with stout. Serve.

Another cocktail made with beer is the Black and Tan or the half and half.

Black and tan (half and half)

8–10 ounces stout
8–10 ounces pale ale

Pour pale ale into a pint glass, then float stout on top. Serve.

The French Connection, the Godfather, and the Godmother are simple cocktails that have amaretto in common. The difference is the spirit.

The french connection versus the godfather (and godmother)

1 ounce cognac
1 ounce Disaronno

Add ice to an old-fashioned glass to chill the glass.
Add cognac and Disaronno and stir. Serve. For the
Godfather, replace the cognac with Scotch whiskey.
For the Godmother, replace the cognac with vodka.

A rusty nail is a weapon that a mobster might use to terrorize someone or to send a message. This rusty nail is delicious.

USTY NAIL

1 ½ ounces Scotch whiskey
¾ ounce Drambuie
Lemon twist

Add ice to an old-fashioned glass to chill the glass. Pour in the Scotch and Drambuie. Stir and garnish with lemon twist. Serve.

A boomerang is a silent weapon that returns to the thrower if it does not hit its target. This drink always hits the mark.

OOMERANG

¾ ounce Jägermeister
¾ ounce bourbon

Chill a shot glass. Pour in the Jägermeister, then float the bourbon on top. Serve.

BIBLIOGRAPHY

Amis, Kingsley. *Everyday Drinking*. New York: Bloomsbury, 2008.

Arthur, Stanley Clisby. *Famous New Orleans Drinks and How to Mix 'Em*. Gretna, LA: Pelican, 1937, 1944, 1965, 1972, 2013.

Bullock, Tom. *The Ideal Bartender*. Saint Louis: Buxton & Skinner, 1917.

Burke, Harman Burney. *Burke's Complete Cocktail and Drinking Recipes with Recipes for Food Bits for the Cocktail Hour*. New York: Books, 1936.

Cawthorne, Nigel, and Colin Cawthorne, eds. *The Mafia: First-Hand Accounts from Inside the Mob*. Old Saybrook, CT: Konecky & Konecky, 2009.

Crockett, Albert Stevens. *The Old Waldorf-Astoria Bar Book*. New York: Crockett, 1935.

Daly, Tim. *Daly's Bartenders' Encyclopedia*. Worcester, MA: Tim Daly, 1903.

Dick, Erma Biesel. *The Old House: Holiday and Party Cookbook*. New York: Cowles Book, 1969.

Duecy, Erica. *Storied Sips: Evocative Cocktails for Everyday Escapes, with 40 Recipes*. New York: Random House, 2013.

Embury, David. *The Fine Art of Mixing Drinks: The Classic Guide to the Cocktail*. New York: Mud Puddle Books, 2008.

Federle, Tim. *Tequila Mockingbird: Cocktails with a Literary Twist*. Philadelphia: Running Press, 2013.

Gabree, John. *The Pictorial Treasury of Film Stars: Gangsters from Little Caesar to the Godfather*. New York: Galahad Books, 1973.

Haigh, Ted (a.k.a. Dr. Cocktail). *Vintage Spirits and Forgotten Cocktails: From the Alamagoozlum to the Zombie and Beyond*. Beverly, MA: Quarry Books, 2009.

Hamm, Richard F. *Shaping the Eighteenth Amendment: Temperance Reform, Legal Culture, and the Polity, 1880–1920*. Chapel Hill: University of North Carolina Press, 1995.

Hearn, Lafcadio. *La Cuisine Creole: A Collection of Culinary Recipes, from Leading Chefs and Noted Creole Housewives, Who Have Made New Orleans Famous for Its Cuisine*. New Orleans: Hansell, 1885.

Helmer, William J. *Al Capone and His American Boys: Memoirs of a Mobster's Wife*. Bloomington: Indiana University Press, 2011.

Hess, Robert. *The Essential Bartender's Pocket Guide: Truly Great Cocktail Recipes*. New York: Mud Puddle Books, 2009.

Jackson, Michael. *Michael Jackson's Bar and Cocktail Companion: The Connoisseur's Handbook*. Philadelphia: Running Press, 1994.

Johnson, Harry. *Harry Johnson's 1882 New and Improved Bartender's Manual and a Guide for Hotels and Restaurants*. Newark, NJ: Charles E. Graham, 1882, 1934, 2008.

Kappeler, George J. *Modern American Drinks: How to Mix and Serve All Kinds of Cups and Drinks*. New York: Merriam, 1895, 2008.

Kobler, John. *Ardent Spirits: The Rise and Fall of Prohibition*. New York: Da Capo, 1973.

Kosmas, Jason, and Dushan Zaric. *Speakeasy: Classic Cocktails Reimagined, from New York's Employees Only Bar*. Berkeley: Ten Speed, 2010.

LeVien, Douglas Jr. *The Mafia Handbook: Everything You Always Wanted to Know about the Mob but Were Afraid to Ask*. New York: Penguin, 1993.

Lipinski, Bob, and Kathie Lipinski. *The Complete Beverage Dictionary*, 2nd ed. New York: Van Nostrand Reinhold, 1996.

Meehan, Jim. *The PDT Cocktail Book: The Complete Bartender's Guide from the Celebrated Speakeasy*. New York: Sterling Epicure, 2011.

Miller, Dalyn, and Larry Donavan. *The Daily Cocktail: 365 Intoxicating Drinks and the Outrageous Events that Inspired Them*. Gloucester, MA: Fair Winds, 2006.

New York Bartenders' Association. *Official Handbook and Guide*. New York: New York Bartenders' Association, 1895.

Okrent, Daniel. *Last Call: The Rise and Fall of Prohibition*. New York: Scribner, 2010.

Reed, Ben. *Ben Reed's Bartender's Guide*. New York: Ryland Peters & Small, 2006.

Reekie, Jennie. *The London Ritz Book of Drinks: From Fine Wines and Fruit Punches to Cocktails and Canapes*. London: Ebury, 1990.

Rosenbaum, Stephanie. *The Art of Vintage Cocktails*. New York: Egg & Dart, 2013.

Schmid, Albert W. A. *The Kentucky Bourbon Cookbook*. Lexington: University Press of Kentucky, 2010.

Schmid, Albert W. A. *The Manhattan Cocktail: A Modern Guide to the Whiskey Classic.* Lexington: University Press of Kentucky, 2015.

Schmid, Albert W. A. *The Old Fashioned: An Essential Guide to the Original Whiskey Cocktail*. Lexington: University Press of Kentucky, 2013.

Stanforth, Deirdre. *The New Orleans Restaurant Cookbook: The Colorful History and Fabulous Cuisine of the Great Restaurants of New Orleans*. Garden City, NY: Doubleday, 1967.

Thomas, Jerry. *Bar-Tenders Guide: Containing Receipts for Mixing.* New York: Dick & Fitzgerald, 1887, 2008.

Trader Vic. *Trader Vic's Bartender's Guide*, rev. ed. Garden City, NY: Doubleday, 1947, 1972.

Wellmann, Molly. *Handcrafted Cocktails: The Mixologist's Guide to Classic Drinks for Morning, Noon and Night*. Cincinnati: Betterway Home, 2013.

Wondrich, David. *Imbibe!* New York: Perigee, 2007.

ALBERT W. A. SCHMID is a Gourmand Award winner and author of several books, including *The Old Fashioned: An Essential Guide to the Original Whiskey Cocktail*, *The Manhattan Cocktail: A Modern Guide to the Whiskey Classic*, and *The Hot Brown: Louisville's Legendary Open-Faced Sandwich*.

NOAH ROTHBAUM is author of *The Art of American Whiskey* and editor of the Daily Beast's Drink + Food section.

CPSIA information can be obtained
at www.ICGtesting.com
Printed in the USA
LVHW071755111121
703076LV00005B/468